Legacy of Leadership
Zenon C.R. Hansen
*"Lead, follow or get out of the way
– make a difference."*

By Steve Myers

Copyright 2014 by Stephen J. Myers, Earl L. Wright,
and The Zenon C.R. Hansen Foundation.
The authors retain sole copyright to
their contributions to this book.
All rights reserved.
Published 2014.
Printed in the United States of America.

All rights reserved. No portion of this book may be reproduced, stored in a retrieval system, or transmitted in any form or by any means – electronic, mechanical, photocopy, recording, scanning, or other – except for brief quotations in critical reviews or articles, without the prior written permission of the authors.

ISBN 978-1-937862-75-6

Library of Congress Control Number 2014907421

This book was published by BookCrafters,
Parker, Colorado
http://bookcrafters.net
bookcrafters@comcast.net

This book may be ordered from
www.bookcrafters.net and other online bookstores.

For my wife Sheryl Bollinger, and my kids, Ben and Jessi Myers. They inspire me every day to "make a difference."

Foreword

Some people are dealt bad hands in life, and their characters are tested and built in such situations.

Zenon Hansen's mother and father abandoned him after meddling family members encouraged his parents to divorce shortly after he was born. As a young divorcee, Zenon's mother chose to let her sisters raise him while she pursued a new life and career. Seldom, if ever, did Zenon see his mother again: not a very encouraging beginning to one's life.

But this unusual childhood allowed Boy Scouting to enter Zenon's life and become the foundation of his strong character and leadership. The generosity and kindness of one man and his sons in a Sioux City Scout Troop allowed Zenon to see the possibilities of his imagination and intelligence. Always a good student but not knowing the full potential of his capabilities, Zenon found Scouting as the outlet to achieve and experience leadership.

This is the story of Zenon's uninhibited desire to succeed and help others achieve their full potential regardless of their social or economic circumstances. We all have faults. However, the real measure of success in Zenon's mind was not that faults had to be corrected, but how you reached your full human potential considering the uniqueness of who you were.

I knew Zenon for two decades. He was a leader, friend, supporter, industrial innovator, entrepreneur, community advocate and maverick for good causes. Being popular was not his highest priority, however, "making a difference" in the world was.

This book has a special message for each of us. Zenon's life story will leave all of us with something to reflect on in our own efforts to "make a difference."

Earl L. Wright

A Spirit Lives On

Amid the rolling rangeland and cornfields of southeastern Nebraska sits a small boomerang-shaped lake surrounded by 300 acres of trees, brick buildings and 1,100 students searching for wisdom, experience and their futures.

This is Doane College and the home of the Hansen Leadership Program.

A spirit dwells here amid the promise and enthusiasm of youth, the legacy of a man from a broken home and humble beginnings who never went to college but loved education, who never had much money growing up but made millions, a man who simply tried to do a good turn daily and wound up helping countless thousands less fortunate than himself.

He had an unusual name, which was fitting because he was an unusual man. He was a captain of industry, master motivator, proud patriot, tireless community activist and generous philanthropist. But above all, he was a Boy Scout, one of the greatest who ever lived. Even though he died decades ago, he lives on at Doane, still fulfilling his boyhood oath – to help others at all times – and empowering America's next generation of leaders.

His name was Zenon C.R. Hansen.

Publicly, he lived what seemed a charmed life. Professional success followed him like his shadow. Still he had regrets. He made mistakes in his private life that haunted him. He rarely talked about them. His public image and legacy remained important to him throughout his life. He guarded them like the bulldog he became. Still, he was a child of religious scandal.

Zenon, age 6, was raised by his maternal grandmother and two aunts after his parents split up before his fourth birthday.

Virtual Orphan

Zenon Clayton Raymond Hansen, pronounced Zen-un, entered this world on Sunday, July 23, 1909, in Hibbing, Minnesota.

> *That same year, William Howard Taft was president. The first Lincoln head penny was minted. The Wright brothers delivered the first military airplane to the Army. The federal income tax was created with the 16th Amendment. And the Pittsburgh Pirates led by shortstop Honus Wagner beat outfielder Ty Cobb and his Detroit Tigers to win the sixth World Series ever played. Over the ensuing years, Hibbing was hometown to several other notables, including New York Yankees slugger Roger Maris, singer-songwriter Bob Dylan, and NBA Hall of Famer Kevin McHale.*

Zenon's father Nels, short for Nelson Christian Martin Hansen, was the Michigan-born son of Swedish immigrants attracted to the booming mining industry in the Hibbing area. The community of nearly 9,000 sat amid the Iron Range, an ore-rich swath of northeastern Minnesota dotted with massive open-pit mines. Hibbing is about 75 miles northwest of Duluth and Lake Superior. At the turn of the 20th Century, Swedes, Finns, Croats and other immigrant groups flocked by the thousands to the region for jobs where muscle counted more than language skills.

Nels was a tailor and his bride Ivah Delle Raymond was a housewife of Irish and French-Canadian decent. They were well enough off in 1910 to keep a live-in servant. But the Hansens were a scandalous couple because she was Catholic and he was Protestant. Her family didn't approve of the match, but Nels and Ivah had eloped three years earlier and tried to make a go of it. From the start, Ivah was concerned with creating a unique identity for her family and particularly her newborn son. She had changed the spelling of her husband's last name from Hanson to the less common Hansen to make it distinct from others with the same name. She picked an even less common first name for her son.

"My mother decided I should have an unusual name. So she chose Zenon," he said, describing how she saw the name in a book and believed it would further differentiate her son from all the other Scandinavian Hansens and Hansons in Hibbing.

He disliked the moniker as a boy but came to appreciate its unforgettable nature as an adult. For 60 years he thought it was unique, but after making national news in the early 1970s, he learned the world contained a handful of others with the first name Zenon. They contacted him after reading his name in the papers, "We are thinking of forming a Big Z or Zenon club and trying to find out how many people there are by that name," he joked.

An ancient Greek word meaning "gift of Zeus," the name can be traced back to about 300 B.C. and Zeno of Cyprus, the founder of the Stoic school of philosophy, which maintains that tranquility can only be achieved by indifference to pain and pleasure.

It took a bit of stoicism for Zenon to endure his early childhood. He grew up a virtual orphan.[1] His mother and father split up before he was old enough for school. He hardly knew them.

---

[1] **Hansen, Zenon C.R.** Personal memo regarding his early childhood and refuting a genealogist's contention in a newspaper article that he was a descendent of John Hanson of Maryland, first U.S. president in 1781 under the Articles of Confederation. Held by Doane College, Crete, Nebraska.

"My mother was the youngest of four daughters," Zenon discovered when talking to an old family friend some 60 years after his parents' breakup. "In addition to being the youngest, she was considerably the most intelligent, attractive and poised of the four. Jealousy existed between the sisters."

Zenon learned that his parents' differing faiths rankled his mother's family, who believed in one ironclad rule, "A Catholic should not marry a Protestant and vice versa."

"My mother being of Catholic-faith ancestry and my father a Protestant, their marriage projected quite a family affair," Zenon said. "A strong-willed grandmother, with the help of three jealous sisters, had my mother and father separated by the time I was 4 years old."

His maternal grandmother, Mary Raymond, and two "old-maid aunts" took over young Zenon's upbringing, and they, along with his grandfather, Egnas Raymond, bounced around, living with relatives from Michigan to Florida to Iowa.

"It was an experience, I can tell you," Zenon recalled. "I had my fanny paddled three times a day and 14 times on Saturdays and Sundays. In those days, adults imposed tough, no nonsense discipline, and children were expected to be seen but not heard. Today, they're not only heard but obscene."

Zenon spent his initial grammar-school years in Miami, Florida, before moving to Sioux City, Iowa. He developed his work ethic in those early years, doing chores at home and odd jobs for cash after school and on weekends.

"I was subjected to strict discipline, both at school and at home, and was expected to mow the grass, carry in the coal, haul out the ashes, and to work and earn everything from a nickel on up. At the time, I resented it, but it was a great background.

"Looking back on it, it was a happy childhood."

By early 1920, at age 10, he was a gangly youth with thick brown hair and blue eyes, living in Sioux City, a bustling community of 70,000 people hugging the banks of the Missouri River. It was a meatpacking center and a transportation hub for river and railroad commerce. Zenon was living with seven other relatives, including his maternal grandparents and two aunts. A decade earlier, his mother's sister, Emma, had married Timothy

Calligan, a railroad conductor with whom they all now lived. However, it was there in Iowa that Zenon's life would be transformed, and his rapid rise to professional success would begin.

At age 17 in Sioux City, Iowa, Zenon showed off his Boy Scout uniform and sash with the record 81 merit badges he earned.

Credo for Life

A train carrying Sir Robert Baden-Powell, a retired British general who founded the international Boy Scout movement, and his entourage chugged into Kansas City, Missouri, on Wednesday, May 5, 1926. It was just one stop on a 17-day U.S. visit to inspect the Boy Scouts of America, which was founded 16 years earlier.

Thousands of Scouts from across the Midwest had assembled, including 126 boys from 22 cities who were to be honored for earning Scouting's highest honor, the Eagle badge. One Eagle Scout had traveled 800 miles from Cheyenne, Wyoming. Another had traveled 275 miles from Sioux City, Iowa. That boy was Zenon, a bright, hardworking 16-year-old who was making a name for himself in Scouting.

Zenon had earned an astonishing 81 merit badges when only 21 were required for the Eagle badge. It was believed to be the record at the time. Merit badges were awarded to Scouts who demonstrated proficiency at skills ranging from first aid to campfire cooking to swimming.

That evening in Kansas City's massive Convention Hall, 5,000 Scouts paraded in front of Baden-Powell, Chief Scout of the World and a British baron. Following the review, James E. West, U.S. Scouting's top executive, ceremonially presented the Eagle Scouts to Baden-Powell. As the general stood, the arena roared to life as the cheers from thousands of assembled Scouts filled the rafters for nearly five minutes. West described the elaborate demonstration in an article he authored for the Scout magazine *Boys' Life*.

"Sir Robert spoke briefly of the world brotherhood of Scouting and then walked down into the arena and personally presented the Eagle Scouts their badges," West wrote. "To these boys, it was the thrill of a lifetime."

A photo showed the Eagle Scouts standing at attention in a column formation. Each wore a smart uniform reminiscent of those worn by American Doughboys in World War I, complete with khaki-colored knickers and long-sleeve shirts, neckerchiefs, knee-high socks and Smoky Bear hats. Baden-Powell walked the rows, stopping at each boy and presenting him with the badge. It was one of Zenon's proudest moments. He frequently told the story at Scout events the rest of his life.

After the awards ceremony, the thousands of assembled Scouts presented a "Kansas City Circus," a demonstration of Scout skills, from starting fire by friction to wall scaling to Native-American sun dances. West described the circus as elaborate, but it was nothing compared to the evening's finale.

"At the conclusion, the hall was darkened and red flares were lighted in four signal towers. The hall became lighted by a soft red glow. A spotlight was turned on the central tower, on the top of which was a Scout with a silk American flag," West wrote. "Quickly, the Scouts came to attention and pledged allegiance to The Flag. Then quietly they bowed their heads and repeated a Scout benediction."

It was a dramatic, grand spectacle – the sort of ceremony and ritual Zenon loved throughout his life. Baden-Powell was a giant of his time and the first of many Zenon would meet in years to come as his Scouting ranks and merit badges were replaced by corporate titles and civic honors.

Zenon discovered Scouting "quite by accident" at age 14 when a high school chum in Sioux City invited him to a meeting after school. His curiosity piqued, he borrowed a Scout Handbook because he didn't have the money to buy one. In it he discovered his creed in the Boy Scout Oath:

> *On my honor, I will do my best to do my duty to God and my country and to obey the Scout Law; to help other people at all times; to keep myself physically strong, mentally awake, and morally straight.*

It changed his life.

"As a teenager, my greatest experience was in the Boy Scouts," he said. "I originally joined because my best friend got me interested in the program. But the real inspiration came from my first Scoutmasters, Jay Keck and Henry Hoskins.

"The way they conducted themselves, and gave of themselves to young people created an enormous amount of respect and admiration in me."

Hoskins first took notice of Zenon because of his dedication, perseverance, and hard work.

"I was chairman of the Court of Honor of the Sioux City Boy Scouts Council," Hoskins said, "and Hansen kept appearing for more merit badges beyond the 21 required for Eagle Scout – a total of 81 merit badges! That's more than any other Scout I've ever known or heard about."

Hoskins got to know Zenon even better when the boy recruited him to be the Scoutmaster of a new troop the boy was organizing. Zenon wasn't old enough to lead the troop but convinced Hoskins to take the lead by promising to do all the work.

Eventually, Hoskins became "Uncle Hank" to Zenon and a father figure. The teen spent an increasing amount of time at the Hoskins' house.

"When I found out that he was being raised by an aunt and grandmother," Hoskins said, "I figured he could use some fatherly advice from time to time. So my wife and I invited him to our house for dinner each Sunday. We had three boys and one girl, and he became just like one of the family."

Zenon felt deeply indebted to Scouting and in particular to Hoskins. They remained close friends for the rest of their lives.

"I was raised an orphan boy and, frankly, I don't know what would have happened to me if I hadn't been in Scouting," Zenon said. "Even my first job with International Harvester came as a result of my Boy Scout work."

Zenon struck a pose of sophistication in 1931 while working in Algeria for International Harvester's European affiliate.

Boy Scout to Boy Wonder

Zenon was a young man on the rise in 1927. Everything seemed possible that year.

> *Charles Lindbergh became the first man to fly alone, nonstop across the Atlantic Ocean, from New York to Paris. Babe Ruth hit a record 60 home runs, and his Yankees won their second World Series. It was the Roaring '20s in America. Prohibition was routinely ignored as Al Capone in Chicago and other gangsters nationwide were in their heyday. Everywhere, business was booming as the stock market hit all-time highs. Calvin Coolidge was president, and work began on Mount Rushmore in South Dakota.*

Zenon was 17 years old and set to graduate that June from Central High School in Sioux City. He had been deeply involved in school life. He was a yell king for one of the school's "most successful" football teams, which finished with a 6-2-1 record and regularly packed the old wooden grandstand flanking the gridiron with fans. He was on the debate team, which argued the merits of national farm-relief legislation and whether the United States and Canada should jointly construct a Great Lakes-St. Lawrence Waterway. He was vice president of the Elite Literary Society, a leadership club. He sold advertising for the yearbook *The Maroon and White* and was a member of the Typewriter Association and Hi-Y Club, an organization dedicated to "clean sportsmanship and Christian living."

He also won the lead role in that year's spring play, *A Lucky Break*, the story of a business tycoon who returns to his hometown after 20 years to build a great factory but runs into a series of amusing difficulties related to a girl he falls in love with. In some ways, the role foreshadowed Zenon's life to come. Henry Hoskins, Zenon's Boy Scout mentor, noted the irony when recalling the play some 40 years later and telling Zenon in a letter how proud he was of the man's performance in the play and life.

Zenon parlayed his school activities along with his Scouting achievements and excellent grades to earn an academic scholarship to attend the University of Iowa in the fall. He planned to become either a physician or a professional Scout executive. But first he would spend one last summer in the sun as assistant director at a Boy Scout camp.

Life was good. His path was seemingly mapped out.

Then came a call from his high school principal, "The manager of International Harvester wants to talk to you."

"What about?" asked Zenon.

"I think he wants to hire you."

Zenon's achievements had drawn the notice of Edmond Burke, manager of International Harvester Company's factory branch in Sioux City. Founded with the 1902 merger of five farm equipment businesses, the Chicago-based company by 1927 had evolved into the nation's leading manufacturer of farm tractors and also had started building trucks. Burke did indeed offer Zenon a summer job, but the teen turned it down because he had already committed himself to working at the Boy Scout camp that summer, and he was a man of his word. Burke understood and asked the young man to come and see him when the camp was over. Zenon did, and the pair had a serious conversation. Zenon expressed his desire to attend college. Burke told Zenon he could get ahead faster if he went to work for International Harvester. In the end, the teenager agreed to postpone college in return for some practical work and business experience.

"The truck industry was new and intriguing to a young man," Zenon recalled.

That August he started his first full-time job. He worked in the Sioux City factory's parts department for $17.50 a week or $910 a year, which is equivalent to about $21,100 annually in 2013. After several months, he was promoted to bookkeeper/clerk/typist. Before his first anniversary with International Harvester, he was selected for a management-training program. College was put on hold permanently.

"And so, at the age of 18, I decided to become a 'truck man,'" he said.

Forty-five years later, a magazine reporter asked Zenon what was the smartest decision he ever made. He replied, "I think it was when I decided as a young man not to do what I started out to do – work for a while and then go to college – but to keep on working."

International Harvester's management program was rigorous and designed to give trainees technical know-how through on-the-job training at its plants throughout the Midwest. There was little if any classroom work. It was hands-on.

"As a part of my training in the Chicago plant," Zenon said, "I was told I had to put together a partially knocked-down tractor – a tractor in the same condition of assembly as it would be when uncrated overseas, with the wheels and a few other things taken off.

"Well, I didn't have too much trouble with that, and I was pretty pleased with myself. Then they told me I had to take it apart, disassemble it completely, and then put it back together again. All of a sudden, I realized I wasn't quite as clever as I thought."

But International Harvester executives thought he was quite clever. After completing management training, he was tapped again for promotion. This time he was one of three selected from among 500 applicants for assignment to the company's fledgling European operations. In April 1929, he boarded a ship for the Old World. He was just 19 years old and had been with the company less than two years.

Zenon knew it was a great opportunity, but after arriving in Europe he realized it would be much more difficult than he initially thought because he only spoke English. So he did what he did best, he went to work. He spent much of his free time studying. First he learned French, and later Italian and German. He also enrolled in a series of home-study courses that he believed would make him more valuable. He finished courses in auditing, accounting, and business management. He also studied automotive engineering.

Again, his hard work paid off. He spent seven years in Europe and North Africa doing a little of everything, from accounting to sales. For fun, he rode horses and began lifelong affairs with gourmet dining and pipe smoking. He spent time in France, England, Belgium, Algiers, and eventually Switzerland, where in 1931 at age 21 he was named comptroller of the International Harvester affiliate. But business lessons weren't the only ones he learned.

He watched firsthand as the Great Depression in 1929 spread from America to Europe. The economic crash impoverished millions of people and sowed the seeds of discontent that allowed fascism to flourish, culminating in Adolf Hitler's dictatorship in Germany and Benito Mussolini's in Italy, and eventually led to World War II. He saw great cultures and societies disappear because of their indifference to the evils of fascism. As soon as Hitler came to power in 1933, his Nazi regime began building detention facilities. At first, these centers housed political opponents and other so-called "enemies of the state" but soon transformed into concentration camps dedicated to slave labor and the extermination of all European Jews. Millions died in the camps.

"It was an exciting but sobering experience," Zenon said, "for I realized that if these dictatorships were not brought to heel, the United States was going to find itself in a war again, just as surely as night follows day.

"When I returned to the United States, I learned that many prominent figures in business, industry and the military shared my views, but that far more prominent and influential individuals did not! The prevailing mood was strongly isolationist. Very few people took Hitler seriously ... ."

These were profound lessons that he never forgot.

"Zenon learned not to be intimidated," said longtime friend Tom Haggai, a retired Baptist minister turned professional speaker, who since 1976 has been executive chairman of IGA Inc., an alliance of thousands of independent grocery stores worldwide. "He saw misdirected leadership and ruthless leadership that harmed innocent people.

"Europe taught him to stand up for what he believed in, even the most unpopular of causes."

Besides business success and profound life lessons, Zenon discovered one more thing in Europe. On May 27, 1933, the 23-year-old executive married 21-year-old Margaretha Marti, a Swiss national, in a civil ceremony at the U.S. consulate's office in Zurich. It was a short-lived affair. When Zenon returned to the United States in the fall of 1935, he listed his marital status as divorced.

He rarely spoke about his past marriages, particularly his first. Close friends later in life, and even his fourth wife, thought he had been married only twice before. Whatever the reasons for his reticence, he put the marriage behind him, looked to the future and didn't remain single for long.

Zenon, during his years in Portland, Oregon.

Seeing the Future

Zenon initially worked as an auditor in International Harvester's Chicago home office after returning from Europe. But what he really wanted to do was sell heavy-duty motor trucks. He was certain it would be a growth industry. He soon got his chance, and after a stint as a commission retail salesman in Gary, Indiana, he was promoted to national fleet salesman.

A lot of people thought he was wasting his career in trucks. Railroads dominated the long-haul freight industry at the time. The country was in the midst of the Great Depression, and the national highway system was a patchwork of narrow two-lane roads with stoplights and stop signs in every town. Long-distance automobile travel was slow. Construction of an interstate freeway system wouldn't start for 20 years.

"In those early days," he recalled, "I was told that there was no future in the truck business – farm equipment was supposed to be the great growth industry – and that trucks were just a sideline which might even be abandoned. But as inexperienced as I may have been, I thought trucks and trucking had a great future in this country, and I decided to stay with it."

He saw opportunity.

"Only the motor truck could offer direct point-to-point delivery from origin to destination," he said. "Best of all, product could be moved at the convenience of the shipper rather than the convenience of the railroad."

While in the Chicago area, he married for a second time, this time to an older woman. Lillian was a native of Illinois and a high school graduate who was four years his senior. She liked to sing and frequently was a guest soloist at church gatherings of many faiths. The couple welcomed a son into their lives around 1938 with the birth of Zenon Raymond Mauritz Hansen. He would be Zenon's only child. Father and son would disappoint each other immensely.

By 1940, Zenon was 31 years old, working 44 hours a week as a national fleet salesman and earning $3,000 annually, equivalent to $49,000 in 2013. Again he was noticed and promoted. This time he was sent to International Harvester's factory branch in Portland, Oregon, as manager in 1941. Within two years, he was named assistant district manager for a territory that included all of Oregon and southwestern Washington. He also became the chairman of the Oregon chapter of the Society of Automotive Engineers, proving his European self-education had paid off. He was making a name for himself again and in more ways than business.

"I had only been in Portland for a short time when the Japanese attacked Pearl Harbor, and like it or not, we were in World War II," recalled Zenon, who served as an officer in the U.S. Naval Reserve during the conflagration. "That's when I made myself pretty unpopular on the West Coast. I had seen the rise in fascism in Germany and Italy, and for the first time in my life I was ashamed of my country."

Fearing a coastal invasion by the Japanese in 1942, the U.S. government forcibly relocated 110,000 people of Japanese ancestry who lived on the Pacific Coast, including thousands from Portland, to internment camps inland. Nearly two-thirds were native-born Americans. They could only bring what they could carry, so most sold their land and other property for a pittance. Estimated property loss was $1.3 billion and net income loss was $2.7 billion. It wasn't until 1983 that a federal commission recommended apologizing to survivors and paying reparations.

"The government was not only interring Japanese aliens but also naturalized Japanese-Americans, and even native-born Americans of Japanese descent," Zenon said. "Japanese ancestry notwithstanding, these people were American citizens, and the government was confiscating their property and incarcerating them in what amounted to concentration camps.

"And I couldn't keep my mouth shut.

"I said, 'You can't do this in the name of expediency. You are suspending the Constitution and stripping these people of their civil rights, and if you can do it to this group and get away with it, then none of us are safe because sooner or later it will become expedient to do this to some other group.'

"Well, the fact remains that they did do it – I was practically a minority of one – and a good many people wanted me tarred and feathered, or tried for treason.

"This was a classic example of how expediency, aided and abetted by mass hysteria, can triumph over reason and the law of the land. Ever since then, I have remained very skeptical of big government and the power brokers who preach that the end justifies the means."

Despite the righteousness of his cause, Zenon was ahead of his time and speaking out publicly against racism and injustice was bad for business during a global paranoia and war. By 1944, rumors ripened on the International Harvester grapevine that Zenon was targeted for transfer despite 17 years of exceptional work with the company, and he started considering his options and pondering his future.

Zenon pushed Diamond T to build trucks with the revolutionary tilt-over cab.

Rags to Riches

During those first years in Oregon, Zenon met another young man on the rise, Louis Courtemanche Jr. He was three years Zenon's junior and college educated. Courtemanche was the grandson of a French-Canadian immigrant who started out as a day laborer in Yamhill County, some of the richest farm country in Oregon's Willamette Valley. Courtemanche's father was a hardware salesman who eventually bought his own store and became International Harvester's biggest independent distributor in Oregon. The family became wealthy selling farm equipment and later in banking. They always kept an eye out for good investments.

In 1944, they found one in Zenon, who joined Courtemanche as a partner in Automotive Equipment Co. The plan was to sell heavy-duty trucks; the industry that Zenon was certain would blossom. Courtemanche was president. Zenon was vice president and general manager, and in his first deal, he landed the Portland distributorship for Diamond T trucks.

Diamond T started out as a Chicago shoe company in the 1880s before turning its corner machine shop into an automobile manufacturer in 1905 and then started building trucks exclusively in 1911. Diamond T made pickups, fire engines, tanker trucks, military trucks and heavy-duty freight trucks of all types. Diamond T trucks were known at various times as the "Nation's Freight Car," the "Cadillac of Trucks" or the "Handsomest Truck in America."

Zenon C.R. Hansen

Business was tough for Zenon's company in the beginning. Trucks, parts and fuel were hard to obtain because of World War II rationing. But moving food, weapons and other war materials to West Coast seaports like Portland made motor trucks essential to the fight against Japan in the Pacific Theater. By war's end in 1945, Zenon's company was the largest distributor of Diamond T trucks in the world and remained so into the 1950s.

"Contrary to the dire predictions of many economists, the cessation of wartime production did not bring about another depression," Zenon said. "On the contrary, the economy boomed as never before and with it the truck industry."

By 1950, the nation's housing industry was thriving, thanks in large part to hundreds of thousands of young men who returned from the war, started families and bought homes under a federal program that provided veterans with low-cost GI loans. Demand for Oregon timber to build these homes soared to all-time highs as did the need for trucks to haul the logs out of the state's vast mountain forests and then move finished lumber from riverside sawmills to the new suburbs sprouting up across the country. Also, new chemical fertilizers, herbicides and pesticides coupled with improved irrigation and machinery revolutionized farming in Oregon's fertile 100-mile long Willamette Valley. More and more trucks were needed to haul the crops to and from canneries running at capacity, churning out corn, beans, pears, cherries, and other foods to feed a growing nation.

America's Baby Boom was on. And Zenon was selling the trucks that fed and housed it. He was growing rich.

"Those were great years, the Portland years," he said. "It's one hell of a lot easier and more profitable to run your own business … I was set for life."

He always considered himself a salesman, first and foremost. He had six simple rules for sales success that he shared with his teams wherever he went:

1) Your quota is your goal – reach it!
2) Improve your service to improve your profits.
3) Add a salesman and add sales.
4) Stock trucks regularly – availability makes sales.
5) Sell like hell – every day.
6) Work.

Legacy of Leadership

As his success and wealth grew, Zenon dramatically increased his involvement in Portland civic affairs. He joined the East Side Commercial Club, chairing it for a year, the Salvation Army board, the Rotary Club and several fraternal orders including the Scottish Rite Masons and the Knights Templar of Oregon. He also became active in the dog world, joining the Oregon Boxer Club and chairing it for a year. He and his son even took top breed honors in 1948 at a Portland dog show for a pair of boxers named Ritter Von Oberehnhof and Oberehnhof's Lucky Play.

Nevertheless, his real passion remained Scouting, and he volunteered numerous hours to it, serving as a Scoutmaster, a Sea Scout Skipper, and eventually a member of the Executive Board of Scouting's Portland Area Council. Mayor Dorothy McCullough Lee told him he was "engaged in the most important work he could possibly do."

"I was the toughest Scoutmaster a boy ever had," Zenon said, explaining that he believed children wanted and needed discipline.

In 1949, he was elected to the Executive Committee of Scouting's Region 11, comprising the Pacific Northwest and western Montana. His commitment and dedication were recognized when he received his first two adult Scouting awards, the Silver Beaver badge in 1950 and the Silver Antelope in 1951, both for his "distinguished service to boyhood" at the local and regional levels.

Building a business and being active in the community required time – a lot of it – time away from his family. So despite his professional success and community honors, his personal life was troubled. His second marriage was falling apart.

"He was married to his job, no matter what job it was, trucking or Boy Scouts or whatever," his friend Tom Haggai said. "He was totally focused on it. As with so many people who have the same job commitment, something usually suffers because of that, and often times it's the husband-wife relationship."

Despite the personal failure, Zenon did what he always did. He put it behind him, moved on and looked to the future.

This time the future appeared in the form of two mechanically minded brothers, Anthony and Benedict Murty. The pair owned a Portland machine shop and had already invented a revolutionary axle-drive steering mechanism

Zenon C.R. Hansen

for trucks. They approached Zenon with their latest idea, a truck cab that would swing forward on a hinge away from the chassis to provide mechanics easy access to the engine for service and repairs.

The "tilt cab" idea wowed Zenon, who offered his own suggestions and provided the brothers with a chassis to work on. The prototype was stunning, and Zenon was convinced of its sales potential. He pitched it to Diamond T executives, who were initially skeptical but were eventually persuaded by Zenon to put it into production. The Diamond T Tilt Cab made its debut at the 1953 Auto Show in Chicago, the same venue where Chevrolet showed off its "dream car" – the Corvette. Both were instant hits and made automotive history.

And Zenon was noticed yet again.

"One day, I got a call from Mr. C. A. Tilt, the founder of Diamond T, and he said, 'Hansen, are you so wedded to that business of yours that you wouldn't consider a change?'

"I told him that depended entirely upon what the change was to be, and he then offered me the sales vice-presidency of Diamond T."

Flattering offer, but it had drawbacks.

"A number of my friends told me I'd be crazy to make a move like that," Zenon said. "Among other things, I would be taking a $30,000-a-year income cut… . But the decision was relatively simple – did I want to remain a distributor for the rest of my career, or did I want to try the big league?"

Zenon, right, and his pal, Green Bay Packers football coach Vince Lombardi, both received Silver Buffalo awards from the Boy Scouts of America.

The Big League

A 44-year-old Zenon returned to Chicago in 1953 as Diamond T Motor Car Company's new Vice President in charge of sales and marketing.

That same year, Dwight D. Eisenhower succeeded Harry Truman as President. Richard Nixon became Vice President. Soviet Union dictator Joseph Stalin died of a stroke and eventually was succeed by Nikita Khrushchev. The United States announced the creation of a hydrogen bomb amid growing Cold War hysteria that had spawned the anti-Communist movement known as McCarthyism. Mickey Mantle smashed a 565-foot home run, the longest in history, and his Yankees won their 15th World Series.

To his new job, Zenon brought a zest for sales and a track record of success. He also brought along Juanita Moilanen, his office manager from Portland. A year later, on December 2, 1954, they were married in Chicago. He called her "Pige," short for Pigeon.

A willowy brunette who wore glasses, Juanita was 40 when she became 45-year-old Zenon's third wife. She was born Juanita Kellogg, a farmer's daughter from the windswept prairie of northeastern Montana. She first married John Moilanen, a bookkeeper at a local auto garage, and bore him two children. Leroy was the oldest. Her youngest, Robert, was about the same age as Zenon's only son. During World War II, Juanita and her family moved to the Portland area where she and her husband eventually split up. Zenon helped to raise her sons along with his own.

"None of them has been a problem," Zenon said. "Only one of them (Robert) saw fit to attend college, and then after leaving college, he worked for a few years and decided to return and get his law degree, which he has done on his own. He is now establishing his own private practice.

"The other two are coming along satisfactorily."

Zenon's career was coming along satisfactorily as well. After a little more than a year with Diamond T, he was promoted to executive vice president and joined the company's board of directors. In 1956, when ill health prompted the resignation of Diamond T's president, the company turned to Zenon. So at age 47, less than three years after joining the management team and nearly three decades after joining the trucking business, Zenon reached the top. He was in charge of a company. He was a captain of industry. He was president of Diamond T, one of the largest truck manufacturers in America. But he wanted to be No. 1, so he went to work.

"All of us at Diamond T felt that we had the finest trucks in the industry," he said. But the company needed fine-tuning.

In his initial year as president, he reorganized the management team, added top executives, cut costs, pushed sales efforts and implemented a novel idea for improving worker efficiency and morale. He launched the "Clean Up, Spruce Up, Sharpen Up" campaign.

"As a result, the plant, from shipping room and machine shop to assembly lines, literally sparkled," company literature boasted. "Everything had a place; everything was in its place. Stored material was stored neatly, properly identified and readily accessible via well-maintained aisles. Floors were spotless, even in the area where ... fuel was pumped into the newly completed vehicles."

The program worked, instilling a sense of pride and responsibility in workers. Efficiency soared.

"Product quality shot up, costly production boo-boos plunged down," a Diamond T report indicated. "Company morale was never so high."

Zenon's efforts paid real dividends, too. In his first year as president, Diamond T saw sales grow more than 20% while profits rose an astonishing 800%.

Business picked up speed over the next few years as the nation in 1956 started building an Interstate Freeway System modeled on Germany's famous autobahns. The freeways linked America's cities to each other, east to west and north to south, with ribbons of four-lane roadway unencumbered by stops signs or traffic signals. The interstates unleashed the long-haul trucking industry to compete with railroads. Despite the boon for his company, Zenon's Diamond T found itself in financial straits. Most of the company's trucks were manufactured with gasoline engines, and Diamond T was at odds with the engine's producer. The rift threatened to cut truck production and sales. Zenon looked for an alternative and found one in White Motor Company of Cleveland, Ohio, best known at the time as the distributor of Freightliner Trucks.

In 1958, Zenon orchestrated a merger in which Diamond T became an autonomous subsidiary of White Motor Company. Diamond T averted its production crisis when it got access to White's line of gasoline engines and other truck parts as well as the company's financial backing. Zenon became Executive Vice President of White and a member of its Board of Directors, while remaining President of Diamond T.

White started out in the latter half of the 19th Century as a sewing machine manufacturer that in 1900 began building automobiles, first steam powered and then gasoline. Shortly after World War I, the company cut its auto line to focus exclusively on trucks. After World War II, White found an even tighter niche in heavy-duty trucks and in the 1950s went on a buying spree that gobbled up truck makers Sterling, Autocar, Diamond T, and REO, the latter a truck company started by Ransom Eli Olds, who also founded Oldsmobile. White began manufacturing its trucks under the Autocar label and combined Diamond T and REO into a separate manufacturing division.

In a cost-cutting efficiency move, Diamond T and REO's management and production efforts were consolidated in Lansing, Michigan, where REO had a plant. Zenon headed for Michigan to head up the new division, knowing that as White's executive vice president, he was next in line for the top job in Cleveland. His career goal was clear.

Zenon also reached the big leagues in his other career as a volunteer Scout leader. After moving from Oregon, he served on the executive board of the Chicago and Lansing councils and eventually was named to the executive board of Region Seven, which comprised Illinois, Michigan, Indiana and Wisconsin. In 1959, he was elected to the executive board of the national council of the Boy Scouts of America and then three years later to the executive committee, the select panel that guided the organization. He would remain on the committee for the next 16 years, helping lead the movement that had shaped his life.

In 1962, he received the Silver Buffalo Award for distinguished service to youth on a national level. It was the highest honor the Boy Scouts of America could bestow on an adult. The first one was given to Boy Scouts founder Lord Baden-Powell during his 1926 visit to America. Since then, the honor has gone to U.S. presidents and longtime Scouts, industrial giants and sports legends.

The 1950s also saw Zenon become actively involved in another national organization associated with Scouting, The American Humanics Foundation. It was the brainchild of H. Roe Bartle, a professional Scout executive as well as a professional speaker, businessman, philanthropist, and politician who served two terms as Kansas City's mayor (1955-63). Founded in 1948 by a group of longtime Scouters, Humanics became a coalition of higher education and nonprofit groups dedicated to preparing college students for careers with nonprofit organizations. Bartle started Humanics because he believed that the people running charities like the Boy Scouts were woefully unprepared for their jobs. Humanics, now the Nonprofit Leadership Alliance, emphasizes the integration of "spirit, mind and body in service to others" through college certification programs and professional internships. Zenon was one of the foundation's early supporters, served three years as its president and became an honorary life member.

In Bartle, Zenon found a lifelong friend and a kindred spirit. They revered the Boy Scouts, believed in philanthropy and cultivated a zest for the good life. Entertaining and throwing parties was always a big part Zenon's life.

"He was always a great host," said Haggai, noting that Zenon enjoyed a cocktail or two. "He wasn't a drunk drinker, though. Now Roe Bartle was Scotch-Irish, and after six (p.m.), he was all Scotch and no Irish."

In Lansing, Zenon entertained friends, clients and other guests at soirees at his picturesque 40-acre estate, which was dominated by a sprawling ranch-style home and a backyard lake. He called it Freudenberg II after an estate in Switzerland where he lived early in his career. "Zenon liked good wine," Haggai said, noting that wherever his friend lived he was active in French cuisine dining clubs, primarily the Confrerie de la Chaine des Rotisseurs, which bills itself as the world's oldest and largest food and wine society.

He also started raising Giant Schnauzers and entering them in dog shows. One was named the Giant Schnauzer of the Year in 1964.

Among his close pals at the time were a couple of sports greats, Green Bay Packers coach Vince Lombardi and Michigan State Athletic Director Clarence "Biggie" Munn. Lombardi would lead the Packers to victory in the first two Super Bowls. Munn, himself an All-American football player at Minnesota, coached Michigan State to its first national football title in 1952, and then its first Big Ten Conference title and a Rose Bowl victory over UCLA in 1953.

"That was an unusual trio," Haggai recalled. "They stayed in touch over the years."

Thanks to Munn, Zenon became a loyal Michigan State fan, booster and donor, and in 1963 he orchestrated the single largest financial gift the college had ever seen. White Motor Co. donated an unused 43-acre factory site valued at $340,000 to the college's Athletic Department for use in academic scholarships.

Loyalty to friends was an important trait for Zenon. It was part of the Boy Scout Law that demanded he be *trustworthy, loyal, helpful, friendly, courteous, kind, obedient, cheerful, thrifty, brave, clean and reverent.*

"If you were his friend," Haggai said, "he stuck by you unless you did something egregiously wrong. If he turned on someone, they were done – no longer a friend. You might as well cross it off. There was no going on your knees and asking forgiveness."

Zenon C.R. Hansen

It was in the early 1960s that Haggai first met Zenon. A North Carolina resident, Haggai made his living giving motivational speeches around the country. His clients included General Motors and the Pentagon. The American Humanics Foundation hired him to speak to its board in Kansas City.

"Zenon was sitting down at the end of the table," Haggai said, "and you could just tell, you were supposed to pick on him a bit, so I did, and everybody else was just laughing. He just had that bulldog feel about him, and all his colleagues, these fellow board members, were delighted I picked on Zenon.

"To this day I can't remember what I said. I wish I could. I just remember them laughing and laughing."

Zenon was just under 6 feet tall with a square build, Haggai recalled. He was an immaculate dresser who wore glasses. He was neither fat nor thin. He walked straight and upright. He was energetic and moved rapidly.

"He was a lot of growl with that deep voice," Haggai said. "He was impressive looking. He would make his presence known when he walked into a room ... you knew he was somebody."

After the board meeting, Zenon approached Haggai, who was apprehensive.

Zenon said, "You're going back with me on my plane. I'm taking you to North Carolina," Haggai recalled. "That's how we met. We bonded. We talked a great deal. From then on we were great friends. It was one of those instant friendships."

Haggai said that their initial meeting came shortly after Zenon had faced his own mortality. Zenon was returning to Kansas City from a speaking engagement when he was involved in an auto accident in which four people were killed. He was hospitalized for four months and spent a portion of it in traction. A photo from the time shows him in a hospital bed bedecked with ribbons and bows and cards from well-wishers.

Zenon made friends wherever he went with his seemingly unquenchable thirst to do good turns and help others less fortunate than himself. He even financed his own student-loan program, lending money to deserving young people he met, whether they were the children of his employees or Boy Scouts he mentored. He kept track of the loans in a small personal ledger, and in return all he asked of recipients was that they keep him posted on their progress.

"He had a spiritual side to him," Haggai said. "His actions showed he had respect and a good wholesome fear of God, which we all should have. God to him was helping every orphan and every Scout boy he ever saw."

"He was always for the underdog and maybe even thought of himself as an underdog."

Good deeds and perpetual community service earned Zenon the chairmanship of Lansing's annual Community Chest Drive, a forerunner of the United Way charity. He also remained active in his fraternal clubs, such as the Shriners and Masonic Lodge, and later the Sovereign Order of St. John of Jerusalem, a charitable organization that sees itself as a modern version of the Knights Hospitallers, a Christian society of warrior-monks that formed in the 11th Century to provide Holy Land pilgrims with hospital care and protection.

He was active, successful, prosperous, and happy.

"Once again, after we made the move to Lansing, I thought I was set for life," Zenon said. "Diamond T was moving along in high gear; our relationship with White was excellent; and I had no desire to make another move. I had a beautiful home on 40 acres outside of Lansing, and the greatest group of friends and associates a man could ask for."

He also remained vigilant and unafraid to support underdogs and take on unpopular causes. He found both there in Michigan.

In October 1964, Michigan governor George Romney, father of 2012 presidential candidate Mitt Romney, summarily fired two National Guard generals after a state auditor's report accused them of misappropriation of government funds in a land deal. The elder Romney, himself a presidential candidate in 1964, was fresh from losing the Republican nomination to Arizona Sen. Barry Goldwater months earlier. The generals were mainly accused of selling a parcel of government land and using the proceeds to purchase other land they wanted for a military base. The auditor's report contended the transaction was illegal because Michigan's constitution prohibited government land sales, allowing only land swaps. The report also contended the generals tried to cover-up the misdeed.

Zenon was troubled that the generals were fired without due process of law or even a public hearing. He formed a committee and launched a drive to raise money for the generals' legal expenses. More than $50,000 was collected in just a few months. His efforts made headlines and drew attention to the case. The public pressure from Zenon and his backers prompted Romney to change the firings into suspensions, first without pay and then with, and then eventually to hold a public hearing on the firings.

"We're trying to go about this quietly without causing embarrassment to anybody," Zenon said.

In the end, the Michigan Supreme Court in 1969 ruled that the generals were wrongly dismissed and ordered them honorably reinstated with full back pay.

"For Zenon, it was just another case of doing the right thing, but he had embarrassed powerful people, and it cost him. In the midst of the controversy, Zenon learned that White Motor Company's board was unhappy with his involvement in the public scandal and quietly informed him that he would not be promoted to company president," Haggai said.

"Zenon thought he was dismissed from the company," Haggai said. "He blamed Romney for that – for making that happen."

But Zenon never mentioned his grievance publicly, even though he believed his career with White was over.

"As a matter of fact, I planned to retire in 1967 after I completed 40 years in the trucking industry," Zenon said, reflecting on his time at White. "I thought I had reached the high point of my career...."

But he hadn't. A once-proud bulldog was howling on the East Coast. Mack Trucks needed a new master. It sniffed around and found Zenon.

His desk and office walls adorned with bulldog memorabilia, Zenon often spoke as if the Mack Trucks logo was a real dog from which he took orders.

The Big Dog

Rugged. Sturdy. Pugnacious. American soldiers first nicknamed Mack trucks "bulldogs" during World War I because the tough vehicles would doggedly pull trailers used to treat gassed soldiers through thick mud to victims on the battlefronts in France.

Five Mack brothers started the company in 1893 when they bought a wagon-repair business in Brooklyn, New York. The Macks were the grandsons of German immigrants who farmed near Scranton, Pennsylvania. One of the brothers, Jack, a former teamster and steam engineer, recognized that the horse era was ending and started experimenting with self-propelled vehicles and handcrafted his first automobile in 1900. It was powered by a four-cylinder gasoline engine and had a three-speed clutch transmission. The chain-driven vehicle was actually America's first bus, built to carry 20 passengers on tours of Brooklyn's Prospect Park. The bus was eventually converted to a truck after eight years in the park and lasted 17 years total. Nicknamed "Old Number One," the durable prototype was so successful and reliable that orders poured in. Mack soon outgrew its location and moved to Allentown, Pennsylvania, and by 1911 had 825 employees who built nearly 600 vehicles a year, making Mack one of America's largest, if not the largest, producers of heavy-duty trucks.

Zenon C.R. Hansen

Unlike other fledgling automakers of the time, the Mack brothers never messed around with manufacturing smaller passenger vehicles, preferring from the beginning to focus exclusively on buses and freight-hauling trucks.

Mack revved through the ensuing decades, adding fire engines, tankers and dump trucks to its growing line of heavy-duty vehicles. Reliability and performance defined its products, and the phrase "Built like a Mack Truck" entered the English lexicon. Following World War II and into the 1950s, Mack was the leader among heavy-duty truck manufacturers, controlling about 45% of the market thanks in large part to a revolutionary Thermodyne diesel engine, introduced in 1952, that provided its trucks with more constant horsepower and speed than competitors. As sales and profits soared, an investment company gained control of enough Mack stock to take over with the intent to cash in.

A succession of finance-oriented CEOs without trucking-industry experience were appointed and set about maximizing profits for shareholders. They fired many veteran Mack executives, deferred production-plant maintenance and machine upgrades, and allowed labor relations to wither, resulting in work stoppages and strikes.

Mack's product quality declined and so did its customers. According to company statistics, Mack lost nearly a third of its market share between 1959 and 1964 and saw earnings plummet from $15.8 million to $3.4 million. It was a company on the brink of bankruptcy.

After the U.S. Justice Department rejected a merger with Chrysler, Mack's future looked bleak and many in the industry, including Zenon, expected the company to go under. A desperate board of directors started looking for a new chief executive with extensive truck-industry experience. They zeroed in on Zenon and asked him to rescue the once-proud company.

Friends and colleagues again thought it would be a foolhardy move on Zenon's part.

"Many well-informed individuals advised me that I was taking over a sinking ship, that Mack was too far gone to save, that Mack would either go under or be absorbed and become a division of one of our competitors," Zenon recalled. "But I thought they were wrong. Mack had a great name, a great product, and above all it had the people. All that was needed was leadership."

"In reality," Haggai said, "the decision was a no-brainer for Zenon. His career advancement had been blocked at White Motor Co., and turning around Mack Trucks would prove the folly of that decision. Plus Mack was going to pay him more money."

So on January 7, 1965, 53-year-old Zenon became the big dog.

That same year, President Lyndon Baines Johnson signed into law the Voting Rights Act, guaranteeing African-Americans the right to vote, and the Higher Education Act, creating a national student-loan program for college kids. LBJ also expanded his war on poverty, which led to Medicare, food stamps and welfare, and began escalating American military involvement in Vietnam. The Rev. Martin Luther King led the civil-rights march from Selma to Montgomery in Alabama, Malcolm X was shot in New York City, and 34 people were killed in the Watts race riots in Los Angeles. A Soviet Union cosmonaut became the first man to walk in space. The Beatles released the movie and album **Help!** *The Los Angeles Dodgers won their fourth World Series behind the pitching of 26-game-winner Sandy Koufax. And Zenon's pal Vince Lombardi coached the Green Bay Packers to its sixth NFL championship.*

"I accepted the presidency of Mack Trucks because, quite frankly, it was the most tremendous challenge that had ever been offered to me," Zenon said. "Here was an opportunity to put many of my own ideas into effect, and rebuild a very individual truck company back to the leader of the industry it had been before. In short they were giving me a chance to make the bulldog growl again – and the offer was irresistible."

Zenon had just one stipulation in taking the leash of Mack, "I only insisted that I be given a free hand if I was to turn the company around."

Mack's board gave it to him and, as always, he went to work, initially focusing on restoring morale within the company and confidence outside it. Remarkably, Zenon kept the existing management team and relied on its experience with the company culture to help get things done.

Zenon C.R. Hansen

"There's no substitute for experience," Zenon said, "and together we set out to turn the company around."

He met with group after group of employees, assuring them that there would be no more firings, no more outsiders brought in, and that future promotions would be made internally whenever possible. He met with union representatives and hammered out new labor deals. The company owed millions to suppliers, so he met with them and promised to pay if given time. Mack in turn was owed millions from customers, so he pushed to collect receivables. He worked to increase production, expanding the Allentown assembly plant in his first two months, catching up on long-deferred maintenance, and purchasing new machinery.

In the name of centralized efficiency, Zenon also set about making Allentown, Pennsylvania, Mack's historic home and site of its main production facilities, the company's central hub and HQ. The way he saw it, company executives should be close to the mainstream workers and the products they manufactured. Instead, Mack's top managers were spending way too much time traveling between plant, factory and offices and not enough time actually working. Six months before he took over, Mack had opened a new corporate headquarters in Montvale, New Jersey, in an elegant suburban setting about 100 miles northeast of Allentown. Mack had also recently built a new engine and transmission factory in Hagerstown, Maryland, which was 150 miles from Allentown. Mack also ran its foreign operations from offices in Bermuda, which Zenon derisively called the "country club." He closed it and the new corporate suites in Montvale, and relocated those operations in Allentown. He also considered shutting down the new engine and transmission factory in Hagerstown and building a new one in Allentown, but decided that would cost too much.

Instead, he bought an airplane and launched Bulldog Airlines, a corporate air force to quickly shuttle executives, salesmen and clients between Allentown and Hagerstown and anywhere else in America where they could sell trucks. Eventually, the Mack air fleet included twin-engine planes, jets and helicopters, and Zenon joined Pennsylvania's Civil Air Patrol and eventually rose to the rank of colonel.

"And to further stimulate employee morale, we dusted off Mack's famous, but neglected, bulldog and put him to work," Zenon said. "When you see the bulldog, it immediately means Mack to everyone. I learned a long time ago that when you have a winning card, you play it every time."

The bulldog had been Mack Trucks' official emblem since the 1930s when the company first used them as hood ornaments. Zenon recalled that during one of his first calls as a salesman for International Harvester in the 1930s, he noticed a small Mack bulldog sculpture on the desk of the client, and then he kept running into the icon on calls at other accounts.

"The bulldog kind of created an inferiority complex for those of us in competitive companies because we recognized the great product that Mack manufactured," Zenon said. "The bulldog is more than just a hood ornament. It represents the dynamic approach Mack has to business. It represents the strength and durability of its trucks, and the pride of all employees."

He remembered those feelings when he went to work at Mack and turned the canine into the company's marketing face.

"We came out with bulldog flags, jewelry, wall portraits, decals, bumper stickers, blazer crests ... everything you could think of," Zenon said.

The bulldog became Zenon's personal trademark, as well. He wore bulldog cuff links, bulldog lapel pins, and bulldog belt buckles. He even had bulldog buckles on a pair of white shoes. His tobacco pipes bore the bulldog logo. A newspaper reporter one day counted that he wore at least 19 bulldogs on his person.

"His fly (on his trousers) had a bulldog hanging from it," said Earl Wright, Zenon's friend and longtime financial advisor. "He knew it was worth a ton. Everything he could get a bulldog on, he did."

His office and the den at his sprawling suburban mansion were filled with art depicting bulldogs. No wonder Zenon often talked as if Mack the bulldog was real.

"He's with me every hour of the day," he said, "not only during my working hours but during my resting hours as well. To me he has become a living being. When I goof off, he nips me in the seat of my pants and bites at my heels. When I do a good job once in a while, I can feel his wet muzzle against my hands."

Zenon had the image of the bulldog stamped on silver-dollar-sized brass coins. On the flip side was emblazoned the slogan "You Make the

Difference." It was a team-building idea he borrowed from his pal Vince Lombardi and the Green Bay Packers. Every Mack worker was given a coin and was expected to carry it at all times.

Everywhere Zenon went, he asked employees to show their coins.

"He would say, 'Do you have your coin?'" recalled Wright. "You'd reach into your pocket and show him your coin. If you didn't have it, he fined you. You had to donate a buck or something into the canister for the Christmas Party or something else like that."

"He absolutely believed it," Wright said of the "You Make The Difference" campaign. "And he had everybody believing that 'I'm doing something important here.'"

Zenon's morale boosting efforts centered on the bulldog proved contagious and wildly successful.

"Employee response was immediate," Zenon said. "All of the sudden our people started taking pride in being part of the Mack organization, even as we asked them to work long hours to get the company moving again."

Today, Zenon's effort would be labeled branding, a common marketing practice. "He was really way ahead of his time," Haggai said. "He actually disliked bulldogs. But he knew that was the way to go."

Employee morale was restored, production was up, and operations were centralized and more efficient. But the company still needed an edge to restore it to dominance in the trucking industry. Shortly after taking over at Mack, Zenon had gone looking for it. He approached Mack's vice president of operations, Walter May, and head of engineering, Winton Pelizzoni, and asked what products were on the drawing board. That's when Zenon first learned about the Maxidyne Engine, an upgrade on Mack's highly successful Thermodyne Engine of the 1950s. The diesel-powered Maxidyne and its transmission system, both invented by May and Pelizzoni, offered constant horsepower with only five gears compared to the complex 10 to 15-gear transmissions competitors offered. The inventors were confident the new engine would revolutionize the trucking industry. A prototype had been built and was already in testing, but previous management was reluctant to put it into production because of high manufacturing costs and uncertainty about whether Mack plants and workers could handle a new line. Zenon wanted to see the prototype – immediately.

"Zenon stopped the guy who was driving the truck and said, 'Slide over. Let me drive it,'" said Wright, recollecting a story legendary among Mack workers. "Hansen started driving the prototype around, grinding the gears. People were wondering when he last drove a big rig? When he finished, Hansen jumped down from the cab and proclaimed the Maxidyne ready for production.

"That's gambling courage. That decision bailed Mack Trucks out. He had the courage to face up to the facts of what the situation was, talk to the people who made a difference and to make an incredible decision."

In 1964, the year prior to Zenon's tenure, Mack had $275 million in sales. Two years later, sales hit $411 million, and by 1970, several years after the Maxidyne hit the market, sales soared to $534 million. Earnings skyrocketed from 92 cents per share in 1964 to $4.26 per share in 1966 alone. Mack built assembly plants in California, Louisiana and Canada; installed one of the nation's first computerized inventory systems; and drew up plans for a new six-story world headquarters in Allentown.

Business boomed. Mack Trucks was saved, and Zenon's resurrection work was the talk of the industry. But corporate takeover wolves smelled profit and began stalking Mack, seeking to gorge on the company's stunning resurgence. Ironically, Mack was now in danger because it was too successful. It couldn't build trucks fast enough or borrow enough money to meet the demand.

"Our outstanding earnings in 1966 had made us a prime target for takeover," Zenon said, "and I was greatly concerned that we might be taken over by a conglomerate whose best interests might not coincide with ours."

Mack battled off so many merger attempts that Zenon lost track of the number. At one point, the predators tried to circumvent Zenon and directly approached Mack board members with their offers without his knowledge. To stop the backdoor tactics, Mack's board named him company chairman and chief executive as well as president. However, Zenon realized that he couldn't fend off the corporate carnivores forever and needed the financial security and protection of a larger conglomerate; a merger was inevitable, but it would be a marriage made on his terms.

"Our feeling was that if we had to get into bed with someone, it would be a Park Avenue glamor girl, not a Greenwich Village streetwalker," he said.

Zenon believed a successful merger for Mack would address four concerns and ranked them in order of importance. The merger must be good for:

1) The employees.
2) The dealers; they have $100 million tied up in Mack trucks and parts.
3) The Mack customer.
4) The stockholder.

Financial experts took issue, arguing stockholders should be the top priority. Zenon's response was succinct, "What good is the stockholder's dollar if the employees are not happy, if the dealers are in trouble, if they don't have a customer?"

New York bankers suggested Zenon and Mack might be a good match with the Los Angeles-based Signal Oil & Gas Company, the largest independent oil company on America's West Coast. Principals of the two companies met in the spring of 1967. It was love at first sight.

"You size up your people and pull it out fast," Zenon said, remembering the summit. "We had never met, and we had an agreement in two and a half hours."

The merger was completed a few months later. Mack and Zenon kept complete autonomy, and the parent company – which later became simply the Signal Companies and eventually part of Honeywell International Inc. – promised not to acquire any other truck manufacturer. In return, Mack received the financial backing to ramp up plant expansion, production and sales, and Zenon joined Signal's board of directors.

Thanks to the merger, the big dog got bigger, much bigger as it took a larger and larger bite of market share in the heavy-duty trucking industry. By 1971, Mack was again the top selling diesel truck in America with one out of every five big rigs sold bearing the bulldog hood ornament. Nearly half of all trucks exported from the United States that year were Macks. By the end of 1973, nine years after Zenon took the leash at Mack, he could now howl with pride over the company's record of success:

- Production soared 138%.
- Deliveries boomed 134%.
- Sales skyrocketed 220%, from $275 million to $880 million.
- Shareholders' equity leaped 147%, with return on invested capital jumping from 2.7% to 13%.
- Earnings per share went supernova, increasing by 764%.

"I don't think many companies can match that record," Zenon crowed. "I have been asked many times how we did this. I will say it again, there's no substitute for experience. It all boils down to experience, damn hard work, and good application of effort by the Mack management team. Our talented, dedicated, ingenious Mack people have made a difference... ."

And every employee had a coin to prove it.

The Boy Scouts of America honored Zenon with a special award for his dedication to Scouting.

Distinguished Eagle

As Zenon neared his career crest in the trucking industry, he also was reaching the summit of his Scouting trek, which began in the Roaring '20s as a tenderfoot teenager. One of his original dreams had been to be a professional Scout executive. He had been helping guide the Boy Scouts of America for nearly two decades. He was a member of the national Executive Committee, the dozen men who directed the organization while working with the national Scout Executive, who was a paid employee supervising day-to-day operations. Zenon had served years on many national committees, including ones overseeing finance, personnel and training, and employee benefits. In 1967, he was elected chairman of the Finance Committee and named national Treasurer of the Boys Scouts of America.

He achieved another milestone a year later when he was honored with the St. George Medal in recognition for his contribution to the spiritual development of Catholic youths through Scouting. Zenon was the first living non-Catholic to receive the award.

He was in charge of the Boy Scout's purse strings, but he had another goal in mind for the organization, too. For several years, he had toyed with an idea that might help boost sagging volunteerism among former Scouts. He envisioned a special award for Eagle Scouts who returned to Scouting as adults to mentor new generations of boys and to raise money to keep the institution solvent and growing. The Boys Scouts of America already had awards – the Silver Beaver, Silver Antelope and Silver Buffalo – that were given to Scouters and non-Scouters alike for "distinguished service to boyhood." But Zenon wanted an award that was more selective, just for 25-year Eagle Scouts who had a distinguished record in business or public service and were giving back to the organization.

"You have got to give these people the opportunity to participate in Scouting," Zenon said of adult Eagle Scouts. "They become the future board members and council contributors."

"If they're like me, they'll admit they never would have gotten anywhere in this world if they hadn't been an Eagle Scout."

Many Scout leaders liked the idea but nothing came of it until Zenon became Treasurer and he enlisted the help of close friend and former Diamond T Trucks executive William Harrison Fetridge, who was the Boy Scouts' national Vice President. Together, they pushed the idea through, and the award was created in 1969. Zenon personally designed the badge.

Ten men were selected as the initial honorees in January 1970, but the very first Distinguished Eagle Award was presented to its creator, Zenon. Since then, hundreds of dedicated men have been so honored, including the first man on the moon, astronaut Neil Armstrong; President Gerald Ford; and Academy Award-winning film director Steven Spielberg.

Zenon served as Treasurer of the Boy Scouts of America until 1970, ultimately managing a $38 million budget for the benefit of 2 million boys. Afterward, he continued serving in various roles, including chairman of the national Advisory Council, until his retirement from Mack Trucks. He also was a founding member of the National Eagle Scout Association, which helped keep former Eagles involved, and was honored with the new organization's first lifetime membership.

Zenon, shown here on the 1972 cover of the *Mack Bulldog* magazine, seemed to see the future throughout his 47-year career in the trucking industry.

Bliss and Betrayal

The 1970s provided Zenon's bright career with its zenith but also his personal life's darkest moment.

Mack's president made national news in June 1971 when he announced the biggest truck deal in history. It was also the most controversial.

Zenon had negotiated a tentative $725 million agreement with the Soviet Union to help equip the world's largest truck factory being built by the Communist government about 600 miles east of Moscow. The plan called for Mack and others to provide machinery and technology worth about $700 million to the new plant and about 100 off-highway Mack trucks worth up to $25 million for use in mining. There had been only $100 million in trade between the two nations a year earlier.

The deal and Zenon made the cover of the national *Businessweek* magazine.

But it unraveled in a few months despite the fact President Richard Nixon that year had launched his détente campaign to ease geo-political tensions between the two nations by normalizing diplomatic relations and increasing trade. America and the Soviet Union, comprising Russia and a confederation of smaller contiguous states, had been fighting an undeclared "Cold War" since the end of World War II, and political factions inside and outside the

U.S. government shrieked that Mack would be sharing technology with capitalism's archenemy communism.

Although the deal was initially backed by Nixon's administration, "super-patriots" and "so-called conservative activist groups" eventually intimidated U.S. officials into backing off, Zenon complained after the deal fell through.

"It was just so stupid," Haggai said. "That deal died because of unreasonable Cold War paranoia. It was a tremendous deal, but we were still getting over the (anti-Communist) McCarthy era.

"Nixon distanced himself because he feared the controversy could hinder his upcoming re-election campaign. But Zenon was right. Trading is the way to better relations. He felt, like I do, that trading is one way to make yourselves so important to each other that you have to stay friends. He thought the Russian deal could have led to a whole lot of other things. He really felt that could have been the first step in really solving the Cold War. He really thought he had a coup. Nixon thought he had a coup. No telling what could have been."

Again, Zenon had seen the future but was ahead of his time. The Cold War dragged on for another two decades.

He stepped down as Mack president early in 1972, turning over responsibility for day-to-day activities to a younger man, while he remained board chairman and chief executive, concentrating on his corporate strategy for expansion.

> *That same year, Richard Nixon became the first U.S. president to visit Communist China and was elected to a second term. The Watergate scandal that led to Nixon's resignation two years later began with the arrest of five White House operatives for breaking into Democratic National Headquarters. Arab terrorists murdered 11 Israeli athletes at the Munich Summer Olympics. The last American ground troops pulled out of Vietnam. Atari's Pong launched the video game industry. And the Oakland A's and slugger Reggie Jackson won the first of three consecutive World Series pennants.*

Zenon C.R. Hansen

It was in the early 1970s that Earl Wright first met Zenon. Wright recalled he was on a team pitching financial-planning services for executives to the Signal Companies board when this booming voice from across the table interrupted the presentation, "I want that."

"It was Zenon," Wright said. "And he had the most profitable division at Signal at the time, so he got what he wanted."

Wright recalled later meeting with Zenon for the first time in his Allentown office, which was set up like the bridge of a ship overlooking the deck below, or in this case the top floor of the new six-story Mack world headquarters. Zenon was the skipper. Three or four secretaries were always scurrying about his office.

"Hansen had this big desk and these six chairs lined up in front of it." Wright said, chuckling at the memory. "All of the chairs had their legs cut down. I felt like a kindergartner. He was trying to intimidate everyone. He also had this bell on his desk. He would ring it when he thought you should be done. Ring, ring, ring! 'OK, let's move on.'"

Despite the failed Soviet deal, Zenon remained an unflinching patriot. He objected to student protests over the Vietnam War, resigning from governing college boards and yanking corporate donations to institutions that tolerated such acts. He made sure every Mack truck sold sported on its cab door a 15-by-23-inch decal with an American flag on top and the slogan "Another MACK truck working for a better US" beneath. Each truck also contained a manual for correctly displaying and honoring the flag. He ordered a corporate promotional truck painted like Old Glory to show Mack was an All-American company. He even signed a deal with Evel Knievel, a flag-waving motorcycle daredevil, to jump exclusively over Mack trucks.

The company was at its zenith as it opened an assembly plant in fast-developing Israel, and the research and development department churned out technological innovations to continually improve Mack's trucks. Zenon credited the Signal Companies board for Mack's return to dominance.

"In my opinion, the Mack-Signal merger was the most successful large corporate merger ever attempted," he boasted, explaining that the financial backing Signal provided was important to Mack's success but not the key. "The really significant value has been this, that Mack has been associated with a high-grade organization which has made good on all its agreements. We have kept our autonomy under Signal, and they have not meddled in day-to-day operations of our business."

Wright described how Zenon once walked into a Signal board meeting to discuss bonus plans for the conglomerate's companies.

"They didn't tell him what bonuses were going to be handed out," Wright said. "He told them. This was the parent company of his company he was talking to. He was making all the money for them, so he told them, 'This is the bonus plan this year in my company. I don't care what you're doing in your companies, but this what I'm doing in mine.'"

Zenon likened the Signal-Mack relationship to a successful marriage, "A cynic once remarked that a marriage is like a hot bath – once you've been in it a while, it isn't so hot anymore. My own feeling is that the romance lasts two or three years, and then the marriage settles down and becomes a well-run business."

His business with Juanita went bankrupt in 1973, and they divorced after 19 years together.

"It was not a good marriage," said Haggai, who at that point had known Zenon for nearly a decade but never really knew Juanita. "I would be there (in Allentown) to visit, and she wouldn't come out to meet any of his friends. I only got a glimpse of her. She got put aside pretty quickly in Allentown."

Zenon had fallen in love with Marilyn Benson, a thin and attractive brunette who was Mack's director of client services. She had frequently traveled with Zenon as he courted clients around the country. She was born Marilyn Ann Hallman and was raised in Michigan. Her father worked as a pharmacist and managed a drug store in Pontiac, while her mother supervised four children at home. Marilyn initially married her high school classmate, Velus Benson, a World War II veteran who graduated from Michigan State before managing golf country clubs in Saginaw, Michigan, and Allentown. He and Marilyn had six daughters and a son before splitting up.

Marilyn, the 46-year-old divorced mother of seven, became 64-year-old Zenon's fourth and final wife on December 23, 1973, in Chicago.

"His marriage to Marilyn was a good marriage," Haggai said. "He needed a lot of affection, and Marilyn really took care of him. That's why she could rebuke him and get away with it."

Zenon seemed to have finally found lasting personal happiness as he hit his career apex. He was a captain of industry with vision and drive, a community activist generous with both his time and money, and a patriot with unwavering dedication to the Boy Scouts and the United States. He counted war heroes, sports legends and business tycoons among his friends. He had even met with President Nixon in the White House Oval Office and had stood in the grandstand just behind him when he was inaugurated.

But a family crisis loomed. As retirement approached in 1974, Zenon learned that his corporate bosses at the Signal Companies had received a galley proof of a biography written about Mack's chief executive.

"It was hugely defamatory of Zenon," Wright said, "and accused him of being a homosexual."

The author? His only son and namesake, Zenon R. M. Hansen.

"Zenon was hurt beyond belief, angered beyond belief," Wright said. "And as a result, from that point forward, as far as he was concerned, the kid wasn't alive. He didn't have a son."

The relationship apparently had been troubled since Zenon split up with Lillian, the mother, two decades earlier.

"The marriage to Marilyn must have been the crowning blow for him," Haggai said. "The son was such an introvert. You could just tell when he was around that he wanted Dad, but he didn't have time for Dad, probably because Dad didn't have much time for him. Because Zenon entertained so much, everybody got more attention than he did.

"Zenon had a hard time showing warm emotion. He showed his love by the things he did for you. The relationship with his son was one of his great failures – no doubt."

Now in his late thirties, the younger Zenon had never really decided on a career although he had authored and published paperback books about the history of Goodyear's airships and luxury train travel. He mainly lived with his mother in the Chicago area.

"Zenon thought he was kind of worthless, living with his mother, living off his mother, and not really doing anything to get himself educated or get into business or a career," Wright said. "He was very, very unhappy with him."

Wright recalled how Lillian had pleaded to have the son come live with Zenon late in his career, "to get young Zenon engaged, to get them reconciled." The father took his son on business trips hoping to spark an interest. "The effort obviously didn't work," Wright said, "because the son tried to destroy his father's legacy, and Zenon's image was everything to him. (The son) was bitter and just tried to take it out on his father with whatever skill set he had, so he did some writing."

Zenon R. W. Hansen eventually killed himself when he jumped in front of a commuter train in Chicago.

"When the son died ... there was nothing from Zenon. Nothing," Wright said. "But we all knew there was such a bitterness with regards to what had been done. Can you imagine ... in your last six months before retiring, your son sends a book to the head of your company ... and starts to destroy your character?"

On July 31, 1974, nearly 47 years to the day after he started in the parts room of International Harvester's assembly plant in Sioux City, Iowa, the 65-year-old Zenon left the trucking industry behind and retired.

He hated it – at least initially.

Marilyn Hallman Benson married Zenon in 1973, and they later retired to Sebring, Florida.

Golden Years

"Zenon was really bitter about his retirement," Wright said. "He didn't want to go to his retirement parties."

In those days, executives and workers alike commonly retired at age 65. It was almost compulsory. Haggai said Zenon also had some health issues related to stomach-reduction surgery that prompted him to step down. After retiring, he missed being in charge, being the center of attention and being the host at all those gatherings and parties, Haggai added.

Within a year of retirement, he also found himself hospitalized when the steering mechanism broke on his riding lawn mower, which overturned and caught fire. He broke an ankle and elbow, and suffered severe burns.

To top it off, Zenon watched as Mack began to backslide financially and lose the market dominance he had worked so hard to achieve. Wright blamed the man who succeeded Zenon at Mack's helm, "He was just horrible." Cashing in on Mack's profitability, the parent company Signal sold stakes in Mack after Zenon retired and eventually spun it off as a public company. Mack stagnated for several decades and was acquired in 2000 by Swedish conglomerate AB Volvo.

"After he retired, he struggled to find himself," Wright said. "We kept asking, 'What are you going to do? What are you going to do?'"

He found the Horatio Alger Association. It was floundering financially and proved the challenge Zenon needed.

Horatio Alger Jr. was a 19th Century minister turned popular author who penned numerous rags-to-riches tales extolling the benefits of hard work and persistence. The non-profit association named after him began in 1947 to annually select and honor Americans who distinguished themselves while overcoming adversity in their lives. Zenon was inducted in 1974 and Haggai in 1980.

Administering a college scholarship program, the association suffered several financial crises that Zenon helped quell with his fundraising skills and business acumen.

"He kept Horatio Alger alive," Haggai said. "Today it is the largest need-based scholarship program in America."

"He took no credit for it whatsoever," Wright said, "but if it hadn't been for him, it never would have occurred."

During retirement, Zenon remained active in several national trucking organizations, including one he founded to create a national trucking museum, which finally opened in Allentown in 2008. Zenon was inducted into the Automotive Hall of Fame in 1982.

He also kept his fingers in the corporate world, helping guide a small Midwest food-distribution company, Super Food Service Inc. Zenon had joined its board shortly before retiring at the urging of Haggai. The company had recently hired a new chief executive, Jack Twyman, an NBA Hall of Fame basketball player, sports broadcaster, and insurance agent. He was just 36 and didn't have much corporate business experience. Haggai, also a board member, thought Zenon would be the perfect mentor for Twyman. Zenon brought along Wright, as a financial advisor to the company.

The results of the collaboration were astonishing. In 1972, Twyman's first year at Super Food and the year before Zenon joined the board, the company notched nearly $290 million in sales and $1.2 million in net income. By 1989, after acquiring several other distributorships, sales had soared 586% to nearly $1.7 billion and profit skyrocketed 1,325% to $15.9 million. Forbes magazine rated it the most productive of America's eight publicly traded food wholesalers.

Zenon C.R. Hansen

Zenon eventually decided to give up his mansion just outside Allentown and Pennsylvania's bitter winters and do what so many East Coast seniors did. He moved to Florida. In 1980, he built a lakeside home at the end of a quiet street in Sebring, Florida, smack in the middle of the Sunshine State. It was a relatively modest house, cinderblock framed, finished with stucco, drywall and tile flooring from Sears. Outside there was a pool. Inside, a lifetime of memorabilia filled the rooms.

"He didn't live a lavish lifestyle like his friend Louis Courtemanche in West Palm Beach (Florida)," Wright said, explaining that Zenon chose to retire to the more modest Sebring because he couldn't keep up financially with his old business partner from Oregon whose family wealth was now largely based on banking.

Zenon had made millions during his career and lived large, but he never accumulated much wealth until he stopped divorcing wives.

"We used to joke that every divorce cost him a million dollars – which was true by the way, several millions actually," Wright said. "All of his wealth for retirement he made in his last two years at Mack through stock options and things like that."

Zenon left Mack with $2-3 million and was pretty much unprepared for retirement.

"He never did any tax planning. He never did any astute investing," Wright said. "He was pretty much taken advantage of by his family and friends."

Wright and the company he founded, AMG National Trust Bank, helped Zenon turn his nest egg into $10 million thanks to savvy investing, a disciplined lifestyle and sticking close to Sebring. "Outside of donations to the Boy Scouts, Zenon's personal monetary philanthropy had been relatively modest prior to retirement, although for decades he had given generously of his time and expertise to all sorts of causes," Wright said.

But Zenon opened his wallet more frequently after his move to Florida and his retirement finances grew more secure. For instance, he and Marilyn endowed a scholarship for truck mechanics at a community college and became benefactors of a local community theater group, helping the Highlands Little Theatre build its first playhouse. The grateful troupe started calling its annual acting awards "Zenons." The Hansens also continued to donate their time and expertise. Marilyn enjoyed delivering meals to housebound seniors and performing other volunteer activities, Haggai recalled, while Zenon made himself a hero to the neighborhood "widow ladies" with his financial advice.

One day in 1990, Haggai decided to stop in Sebring and see his old pal, who had been battling health problems for several years, and was startled by the scene he encountered.

Even though he was expected, no one answered the door for Haggai, who walked in anyway. No lights were on anywhere. Zenon was sitting in the middle of a dark, silent room, just staring into oblivion, Haggai said, calling it a very sad and surreal scene of loneliness.

"He was feeling neglected," Haggai said. "I could tell then that he was a hurting person."

As the old friends chatted, Haggai found that Zenon had become more spiritual and introspective. He was dying of leukemia.

A magazine reporter once quizzed Zenon about his biggest mistake, "Probably that I have not devoted enough time to personal affairs, particularly financial. I have devoted a great proportion of my time to civic affairs and my businesses. But I'm going to get along all right. I have had a great deal of personal satisfaction working with and helping people, so I'm not going to worry about it."

Haggai believed Zenon was performing a more in-depth assessment of his life – the achievements and the mistakes – in his waning days.

"I'm sure sitting there in the dark, he thought about it," Haggai said. "He didn't have a namesake, and he could have had a namesake. He could have had grandchildren. It's a funny thing, he really liked young people, but he wouldn't have been goofy about grandchildren. He wasn't geared to be a family type, and why should he be? He had no close ties growing up as a boy. He was all on his own. He talked about those two unmarried aunts, but they didn't raise him. He did it.

"That was the dark side of Zenon, that he didn't build a family, and he had multiple wives. He was the greater loser for that.

"But on the whole," Haggai continued. "Zenon led an exemplary life. I can't think of anything he did wrong, that he did outright wrong. Perhaps he had some secret things… . Could he have blunders? Certainly he did. It certainly is true his domestic life was one he wasn't proud of. But his basic moral principles were sound.

"His actual moral conduct was as good as any business executive I have known, and I've known some mighty fine ones. I can't think of any time that he would compromise on a moral principle. I don't know any guy whose moral instincts were any better."

Zenon C.R. Hansen died on October 19, 1990. The old Scout was 81.

That same year, George H. W. Bush was president and ordered U.S. forces to attack Iraq when Saddam Hussein invaded neighboring Kuwait. East and West Germany reunited, Poland held its first free elections, and the Soviet Union began disintegrating as the Cold War neared its end with the collapse of the Iron Curtain of Communist governments across Eastern Europe. South Africa released Nelson Mandela from prison after 28 years. The United States launched the Hubble Space Telescope and saw the first episode of the animated TV show The Simpsons. *Led by future Hall of Fame shortstop Barry Larkin and its "Nasty Boys" bullpen, the Cincinnati Reds swept the Oakland A's in four games and won its fifth World Series.*

Zenon's obituary appeared in the New York Times and newspapers across the country. A fortnight later, work stopped at Mack Trucks facilities nationwide as 7,000 employees paid tribute with a minute of silence. At the same time, bells tolled as Marilyn Hansen and 300 friends and associates came to attention in an Allentown cathedral where Haggai led a memorial service. A color guard of four Eagle Scouts marched down the aisle as a choir sang "The Battle Hymn of the Republic" to open the service.

"All of us have some moment in our life that our life is changed," eulogized Haggai, who then and to this day wears a gold bulldog medallion over his heart to remind him of his friend. "He stood with a group of kids. And he raised his hand. And then Zenon C.R. Hansen said for the first time, `On my honor, I will do my best, to do my duty to God and my country. And to obey the Scout law ... .'

"That became his decision factor at every point of his career. He never understood why people talked about Scouting as if it was something for children."

Zenon left behind a $10 million estate that was divvied up between his wife, a scholarship fund run by Haggai, and a family charity that eventually became The Zenon C.R. Hansen Foundation, which was dedicated to advancing his principles and beliefs.

The great lesson of Zenon's life can be found in his simple slogan, *You Make the Difference.* He believed in it so much that he made it his legacy.

"Be a leader or help someone be a leader," Wright said. "His greatest satisfaction came from helping and seeing others he cared about succeed, people like Tom Haggai, Jack Twyman and me. His biggest disappointments came in seeing people he knew could succeed just borrow from and live off the success of others."

Hansen Leadership Hall, the largest dormitory, on the campus of Doane College.

Legacy of Leadership

A life-sized bronze bas relief of Zenon's profile hangs above the entrance to Doane College's Hansen Leadership Hall in Crete, Nebraska, seemingly watching over and assessing all who come and go. It's as if he's still asking questions:

> *Can you work hard?*
> *Will you make a difference?*
> *Are you a leader?*

This is where his spirit dwells, where his legacy lives on, still leading, still helping others decades after his death.

The three-story dormitory, home to up to 175 students, was built in 2000 at a cost of $5 million, $1.5 million of which came from The Zenon C.R. Hansen Foundation. Administered by Zenon's friend and financial advisor, Earl Wright and the company he founded, AMG National Trust Bank, the Foundation has taken an initial endowment of less than $4 million, invested it wisely and ultimately given away about $20 million, mainly funding scholarships and education-related endeavors.

The Foundation is one of Doane's largest benefactors, and Hansen's name pops up everywhere on campus:

Legacy of Leadership

- Hansen Leadership Hall
- Hansen Leadership Program
- Hansen Leadership Awards
- Hansen Leadership Room
- Hansen Scholars
- Hansen Speakers Series

Zenon and leadership are nearly synonymous at Doane, which is about 30 miles southwest of Lincoln, Nebraska. Students talk a lot about leadership. Although people on campus don't know much about him, his legacy is part of the fabric of the college, which is remarkable because he had no close connection to Doane or Crete, a prairie town of about 7,000 people. The fact that he had no college education at all makes it all the more noteworthy.

He initially became curious about Doane after being impressed by a young employee who was a graduate. Wright and his wife Nancy Seacrest Wright, both natives of Lincoln, had been involved in Doane fundraising for decades, and it was those ties that led Zenon to the college.

"He identified with the kids who were there. He saw himself," said Wright, who first brought Zenon to Doane's campus in the 1980s. "They're just good hard-working, common-sense kids with Midwestern values, and they're so malleable. You put them in a good educational environment and good things can happen."

So Zenon, who had no surviving children or close relatives, made sure a large chunk of his estate benefited the small liberal-arts school. And just like that, he had more than a thousand heirs, the students of Doane, and in particular the 150 or so annual participants in the Hansen Leadership Program.

"Our thought was that we would help create a unique graduate," said Wright, "and employers would come to Doane because we've got a graduate for them who is really mature and has a leadership perspective and sense of responsibility that would be helpful to them. We did not care if it's journalism or business ... or whatever."

Charisma, hard work and community service were some of Zenon's hallmark leadership traits. When a problem or need arose in his life, his business or his community, he acted and, more often than not, took charge. Leadership came easily for him.

"Lead, follow or get out of the way – make a difference" was Zenon's motto, Wright said.

The hard-charging Zenon was flamboyant, dramatic, at times loud and even bombastic, but he was true to his word.

"He was a ham, a total ham," Wright recalled. "But he was totally genuine. He wasn't just there to blow smoke at you. He totally and absolutely believed in what he said. He was amazing that way. He wanted everyone to know and believe they could make a difference."

And most importantly, he got things done, whether it was organizing a Boy Scout troop at age 16 or rescuing Mack Trucks from impending insolvency at age 55. For Zenon, leadership meant making tough decisions in a timely fashion, and that often meant taking risks.

"When you're dealing with the future, with the unknown, nothing is laid out in spades – you have to gamble," Zenon said. "Once you recognize this, it becomes a lot easier to make those difficult decisions. For in my opinion, it is far better to take timely action – even if it might turn out to be wrong – than to procrastinate."

People, whether employees or acquaintances, recognized his leadership and responded, making him a success everywhere he went.

"Zenon Hansen is a man of his word," wrote W. C. Parker, a Diamond T executive who first met Zenon in 1944 when he was negotiating to become the company's truck distributor in Portland, Oregon. "He never breaks a promise which is within his power to keep …. He never lets outstanding performance go unrewarded in some way. He has been an inspiration to many. He has never asked an employee to do anything he would not or could not do himself."

Hundreds of similar testimonials are contained in several large scrapbooks commemorating the milestones of Zenon's nearly 50-year career in the trucking industry. The books are housed along with a multitude of other memorabilia of his life – from his many Boy Scout awards to several 2-foot-tall bronze statues of his role models to the dozens of autographed books and photographs of celebrities he met – in the Zenon C.R. Hansen Leadership Room on the fifth floor of Gaylord Hall, Doane College's oldest building.

Perhaps the best affirmation of Zenon's leadership ability came in 1965 when he took over the financially floundering Mack Trucks. Surprisingly, he kept the existing management staff in place.

"Zenon went into Mack Trucks and didn't replace a man," Wright said. "He went in there with the entire team that was failing and had problems, and worked with that team. It was that same management team during his entire 10-year tenure at Mack Trucks."

He also never endured a labor strike during his career, a fact of which he was most proud.

"He knew there were unions and that there was a place for unions," his longtime friend Tom Haggai said. "He didn't want any separation (from workers). He never wanted to be where he would be removed from the aches, the pains, the turmoil, as well as the hopes and dreams of a good job … . That's why he moved all Mack's offices to Allentown."

"Zenon had a common touch with his employees," Wright said, recalling a story told by Mack workers, "There was a guy in the junkyard at Mack who was doing a great job handling scrap, and Zenon one day drove his Cadillac out to the junk yard and asked the guy to get down from whatever he was doing and handed him his bonus check. The guy was shocked. First of all, he had never seen the CEO or president of Mack in his life. Second, he got a bonus, and he didn't even know what a bonus was."

Zenon loved personally handing out bonus checks and the loyalty that simple act inspired.

"The leadership quality I saw most in him was courage. His courage was courage of principle," Wright said, noting that the man wasn't without traits disliked by many. "Hansen was idiosyncratic, bombastic, a pain in the ass, and had an ego as big as the building that he was in, but everybody just worked well together regardless of his personality. He made everyone believe they were the key to Mack's success.

"Not everyone loved him, but they respected him."

"Those people that didn't like him," Haggai said, "he didn't mind because they were the ones who thought they were something, and

Zenon didn't like them because they weren't really doing a darn thing."

Wright recalled the opinion of one key Mack executive, who was supposed to be Mack Truck's president before Zenon's hiring, "He disliked Zenon immensely, but never worked harder, never got better results in his life."

Zenon exhibited his penchant for leadership at an early age. After becoming an Eagle Scout at age 16, he decided to organize and run his own Boy Scout troop in Sioux City, Iowa, but ran into a snag. A scoutmaster needed to be 18 and Zenon was too young. Harry A. Hoskins, who chaired scouting's Court of Honor in Sioux City, recalled how the dynamo Zenon recruited him for the scoutmaster job by promising to be Hoskins' assistant and do all the work. Thus Troop One was born.

Hoskins became a lifetime friend, mentor and inspiration to Zenon, the first of several role models who showed him what it meant to be a leader. Many were famous people that he knew personally and spoke about often:

- **Vince Lombardi**, the coach of the Green Bay Packers and winner of the first two Super Bowls in 1967 and '68. Zenon found a kindred soul in Lombardi, who believed excellence came through total commitment and team effort. Under Lombardi's leadership, many of his players performed at levels previously beyond their expectations, a trait Zenon tried to instill in his management teams.

- **Douglas MacArthur**, the World War II general and Medal of Honor recipient. Zenon saw a man who spoke honestly and openly despite the political and personal risk and always kept his word, immortalized with his "I shall return" vow after the fall of the Philippines in 1942. He was a goal-oriented leader who had a genius for inspiring others to the same convictions.

- **Eddie Rickenbacker**, the top World War I fighter pilot for the United States and a Medal of Honor winner. He was a rare individual who made the transition from war hero to successful business leader. Zenon learned that the same bravery and determination that led Rickenbacker to shoot down 26 enemy planes in six months in 1918 also allowed him to recover from the bankruptcy of his startup automotive company, rise to ownership of Eastern Airlines and become a champion of free enterprise.

- **H. Roe Bartle**, a longtime Boy Scout executive and a two-time mayor of Kansas City, was a boisterous and charismatic leader nicknamed "The Chief." A lawyer by training, Bartle found his calling in public service, public speaking and philanthropy. He was a founder of the American Humanics, now the Nonprofit Leadership Alliance, an organization dedicated to training college students for careers in community and public service.

Zenon saw leadership, as exemplified by his heroes and the free-enterprise system, as keys to success. He thought colleges should be a place where young people were exposed to them but he didn't always see that happening.

"I get sick and tired of hearing that industry hasn't done a good job of selling our educators and students on the benefits of the free-enterprise system," he said. "If these college professors are so damned smart, they ought to know that in many instances the endowments for these buildings they are in, the very campuses they are on, have been created by the blood and sweat of people who never had a college education."

Zenon was one of those people without a degree, but he was a lifelong learner and supporter of higher education. He spurned a scholarship to the University of Iowa to work for International Harvester. But wherever he went during his career, he became involved with and supported local colleges and universities, from Linfield College in Oregon to Michigan State in Lansing to Stonehill College in Massachusetts. He held eight honorary degrees.

In the end, he proved his commitment to higher education with his Foundation's endowments to Doane's Hansen Leadership Program, which totals more than $3 million. The innovative program is dedicated to fostering the next generation of American leaders with six core values:

1) Inclusiveness.
2) Service.
3) Empowerment.
4) Proactivity.
5) Accountability.
6) Integrity.

The program, according to school literature, "gives students the skills and knowledge they need to become strong leaders throughout campus, and encourages them to refine their abilities to serve their community beyond graduation."

Carrie Petr, who holds a PhD in philosophy in higher-education leadership, directs the Hansen Leadership Program, which annually selects about 50 incoming Doane freshman for the Directions Program, a one-year indoctrination effort into the overall leadership program. There's an extensive, competitive application process that requires a 3.2 high school grade-point average and leadership experience either in high school or the community. Prospective students must write an essay reflecting on their leadership experience.

"We're looking for someone who wants to be here and isn't just collecting experiences for their resume ... someone who really has ideas about what leadership is," Petr said. "Leadership is something that goes in all different directions for all different people depending on their experiences. It's a lot like art."

Those selected to the program live in the Hansen Leadership Hall, an exclusive dorm that features suite-style rooms for up to 12 people, attend exclusive workshops to develop and strengthen their leadership skills, and work with upper-class peer mentors.

Freshmen are expected to perform community service for the college or the Hansen Leadership Program. After the first-year Directions tutorial on leadership, students can continue to live in Hansen Leadership Hall but are expected to become leaders on campus in their particular field of study and continue their community service. Many take an active role on the program's advisory board.

"Directions has allowed me to improve as a leader and a student. I get to live and grow with 11 other girls who have similar interests and integrity," said freshman Jessica Brown. "I have also gotten numerous opportunities you can't find in any other group on campus."

The Leadership Program's student advisory board also hires big-name speakers to visit Doane. The Hansen Speaker Series brings to Crete people who exemplify Zenon's commitment to leadership, hard work and community service, people such as film star James Earl Jones, professional basketball player Sheryl Swoopes, and Cornell University professor Steven Squyres, who headed up NASA's Martian rover program. The speakers fill Doane's auditorium with students, faculty and community members.

Another big event sponsored and coordinated by the Leadership Program is Doane's Relay For Life, a 12-hour fundraiser for the American Cancer Society held annually in April. It's a massive carnival-like event that counts Crete townsfolk as well as more than 85% of the student body as participants in the walk relay.

"It's one of the major campus events," said Jay Fennell, assistant director of the Hansen Leadership Program. "They've turned it into the social event of the year."

Students and townspeople bring wads of cash to spend. The event one year raised more than $70,000, earning Doane recognition as the highest per capital fund-raising event among U.S. colleges. "The kids do it all," Fennell said.

There's also the annual Hansen Leadership Awards, nicknamed the Bulldogs after the logo of Mack Trucks. The award, a chrome-plated bulldog hood ornament encased in a glass globe, is given annually to two students and two members of the faculty or staff at Doane who have exhibited outstanding leadership.

There is an obvious pride at Doane among those who are in the Leadership Program and Hansen Leadership Hall. "It feels like a healthy family. The Hansen people feel like they are a clique," Petr said. "They are really proud of it."

So is Petr.

"What we do here at Doane is unique for a school our size and in this region. That the Hansen Foundation has allowed us to have this Leadership Program, it's a gift, and I don't think our students realize it because they don't go to college anywhere else. But all of the faculty professionals here realize that it is really truly unique."

Beside the leadership program, The Zenon C.R. Hansen Foundation funds four four-year scholarships at Doane. Since 1991, a scholarship has gone annually to an Eagle Scout or Gold Star Girl Scout, the highest ranks possible, who best personifies Zenon's dedication to hard work, community service and leadership. Each scholarship is worth about half the cost of tuition.

"I definitely couldn't have done it without the Zenon scholarship," said Cammie Schwartz, who hails from a ranch just outside Mullen, Nebraska, population 450. She credits her mother for her joy in community service, and a Girl Scout leader for showing her that the possibilities in her life were endless.

"Whatever dreams we had, she never told any of us no. She may not have liked some of our ideas. But she never told us no. She would ask how we would go about doing it, and in talking about it, we would usually come to the conclusion on our own that it wasn't a good idea."

Schwartz double majored in computer systems and art with an emphasis in graphic design. Outside of getting a job and continuing her community service, her plans for life after graduation are simple, "I hope I can be the leader that other people have been for me."

Zenon would be smiling.

His spirit lives on in Cammie Schwartz and the other students in the Hansen Leadership Program, principled and dedicated young men and women who want to make a difference – it's the stuff of which leaders are made.

Acknowledgments

Many thanks to Vivienne Benoit of the Zenon C.R. Hansen Foundation for helping shepherd this project through to completion and to graphic artist Juliana Doan of AMG National Trust Bank for designing the book's cover.

But most of all I want to thank Earl Wright and Tom Haggai for giving me the opportunity to tell Zenon Hansen's story. In researching the book and interviewing these two men, who were Hansen's friends, it became readily apparent that Zenon had a profound impact on their lives. They seem to be the living embodiment of Hansen's "make-a-difference" motto. They are extremely successful businessmen who give back to their communities in so many ways and are willing to take a stand for what they believe is right. In writing the book, I discovered that I too want to make difference in the world, even the smallest of differences. I want to be a little more like Earl and Tom, and ultimately Zenon. It's something we all should want.

Steve Myers

Biographical Information
Zenon Hansen's 1982 resume

HANSEN, Zenon C.R. (Clayton Raymond)
Born: Hibbing, Minnesota, July 23, 1909
Parent: N.C.M. and Ivah Delle (Raymond) Hansen
Married: Marilyn H. Benson, December 22, 1973
Children: Zenon Raymond Mauritz Hansen
Schools: Elementary – Miami, Florida
    High School – Sioux City, Iowa
Degrees: Salem College, Salem, West Virginia – D.H. (Honorary)
    Linfield College, McMinnville, Oregon – L.L.D. (Honorary)
    PMC Colleges, Chester, Pennsylvania – L.L.D. (Honorary)
    St. Michaels College, Winooskie, Vermont – L.L.D. (Honorary)
    Gardner-Webb College, Boiling Springs, North Carolina – D.H. (Honorary)
    Stonehill College, North Easton, Mass. – D.B.A. (Honorary)
    Ferris State College, Big Springs, Michigan – L.L.D. (Honorary)
    Hardin-Simmons University, Abilene, Texas – D.C.S. (Honorary)
    Fraternities: Tau Beta Pi – Michigan State University Chapter (Honorary)
    Alpha Kappa Psi – Michigan Sate University Chapter (Honorary)
Church: Presbyterian
BUSINESS
1927-41 International Harvester Company, also International Harvester Export Company, Europe and North Africa
1941-43 Branch Manager, International Harvester Company, Portland, Oregon
1943-44 Assistant District Manager, International Harvester Company, Portland, Oregon
1944-53 Vice President, Director, Manager, Automotive Equipment Company, Portland, Oregon
1953-55 Director of Sales, Vice President, Diamond T Motor Car Company, Chicago, Illinois

1955-56 Executive Vice President, Director, Diamond T Motor Car Company, Chicago, Illinois
1956-58 President, Director, Diamond T Motor Car Company, Chicago, Illinois
5/1/58-1/6/65 President and Director, Diamond T Motor Truck Company, Chicago, Illinois, and Executive Vice President and Director, The White Motor Company, Cleveland, Ohio
1/7/65-3/28/67 President and Director, Mack Trucks, Inc., Allentown, Pennsylvania
3/29/67-2/1/72 Chairman of the Board and President, Mack Trucks, Inc., Allentown, Pennsylvania
9/12/1967-5/1/68 Director, Signal Oil and Gas Company, Los Angeles, California
5/1/68-7/31/74 Director and Member of the Executive Committee, The Signal Companies, Inc., Los Angeles, California
2/1/72-7/31/74 Chairman of the Board and Chief Executive Officer, Mack Trucks, Inc., Allentown, Pennsylvania

DIRECTORSHIPS

Director, Dartnell Corp. 1966-
Director, American Heritage Life Insurance Company, 1971-1978.
Director, Super Food Services, Inc., 1973-

MILITARY

U.S.N.R., Lt. (j.g.) S.C.
    Certificate of Appreciation, 1970
Old Guard City of Philadelphia, Inc.
    Honorary Member
    Brigadier General
    The Centennial Legion Historic Military Commands, Inc.
        The Gold Medallion
        The Gold Medal
Coast Guard League
    Honorary Commander
Michigan Naval Militia
    Honorary Commander, 1969-
Honorable Order of Kentucky Colonels
American Veterans of World War II
    National Leadership Award, 1966
Tennessee Colonel, Aide de Camp
Navy League of the United States (Life Member)
    Director, Lehigh Valley Council, 1974
Society of American Military Engineers (Life Member)
American Ordnance Association (Life Member)
    Vice President – Chicago Post, 1956-63
    Vice President – Michigan Post, 1963-64
    Director, Philadelphia Chapter, 1966-72

Honorary First Defenders, Allentown Chapter
Civil Air Patrol
    Lieut. Colonel, 1969
    Colonel, 1971
    National Appreciation Award, 1969
    National Chairman of Business Memberships, 1969-78
    Pennsylvania Wing Award, 1970
    CAP-NEC Award, 1970
    Exceptional Service Award, 1971
American Legion
    Department of Maryland, Americanism Award, 1970
    Department of Maryland, Citation of Appreciation, 1970
    Department of Maryland, Citation for Meritorious Service, 1972
    Department of Pennsylvania, Distinguished Service Medal, 1971
Veterans of Foreign Wars, Macungie Memorial Post No. 9264
    Honorary Member, 1971
Reserve Officers Association, Lehigh Valley Chapter.
    Distinguished Community Service Award, 1972
Colonel, Staff of Governor of Louisiana, 1972
Air Force Association
    Civil Air Patrol Committee, 1972-74

PATRIOTIC

Invest in America
    President, National Council, 1969-1973
    Chairman, National Council, 1973-1977
    Chairman, Pennsylvania Council, 1969-1974
    Chairman Emeritus, 1978-
Freedoms Foundation at Valley Forge
    Free Enterprise Exemplar Medal, 1970
    Chairman, Committee of the One Thousand, 1970-1974
    Life Associate Member, 1970
    National Trustee, 1970
    Honor Certificate, 1977
German-American National Congress, Inc.
    Honorary Chairman, German-American Heritage Group Conference, 1970
    Gold Pioneers of Space and Rocketry Medal, 1970
    American Citizens Award, 1971
Flag Plaza Foundation, Charter Member
    The American Artificer's Award, 1970
MacArthur Memorial Foundation
    Member of National Advisory Board, 1970-1974
Douglas MacArthur Academy of Freedom
    Freedom Medal 1970

Allentown Flag Day Association (Life Member)
    Honorary Chairman, Committee for Pageant of Flags, 1971
Liberty Bell Shrine of Allentown, Inc., (Life Member)
Hawaii YAF Kuokoa Freedom Award, 1970
COLLEGES, UNIVERSITIES AND SCHOOLS
Trustee – Linfield College, McMinnville, Oregon, 1960-1970
Trustee – Missouri Valley College, Marshall, Missouri, 1963-1971
Trustee – Salem College, Salem, West Virginia, 1962-1971
President – Salem College Foundation, 1962-1971
Board of Development – Hardin-Simmons University, Abilene, Texas, 1971-1976
    President's Club (Life Member)
Board of Advisors, Gardner-Webb College, 1974
Board of Associates – Muhlenberg College, 1965-1971
Board of Associates – Cedar Crest College, 1965-1971
Advisory Board – Lariat Boys Ranch, 1965-1974
Board of Trustees – Foundation for Independent Colleges, 1967-1970
Trustee, Valley Forge Military Academy, 1975-1978
Fellowship of Christian Athletes, 1966-
    Honorary Life Member, 1968
    "Super" Teammate Award, 1970
    Board of Directors, 1970-1971
Michigan State University
    Varsity "S" (Honorary)
    Spartan Award, 1964
    Alumni Association (Life Member)
    President's Club
P.M.C. Alumni Association (Life Member)
Asa Packer Association, Lehigh University, 1969-1974
Belen Jesuit Preparatory School Havana-Miami
    Honorary Alumnus, Class of 1949
Northwood Institute – Northwood Business Leader Award, 1982
FOREIGN
Latin-American Chamber of Commerce – Diploma of Gratitude, 1970
    Director, 1970-1972
Sovereign Order of St. John of Jerusalem – Chevalier, 1972
    Commander, 1973-
Sovereign Order of Cypress – Chevalier, 1972
Sovereign Military Order of St. George in Corinthia, 1973
Knight, International Knights of New Europe, 1977
Chile – Order Bernardo O'Higgins – Officer
Dominican Republic – Santo Domingo, Distinguished Honorary Citizen, 1973
France – Order of Merit and Devotion – Officer
France – City of Paris Bronze Medal

France – Order of LaFayette Medal of Honor, 1974
Honduras – Key to the City of Tegucigalpa, 1969
Italy – Golden Eco Award – Industry, 1973
Italy – Order of Crown of Italy – Knight of the Grand Cross, 1974
Israel – State of Israel Bonds
    Holy City of Peace Award, 1972
Poland – Polonia Restituta – Knight Commander
Europe – Confederation Europeenne des Anciens Combattants
    La Croix du Combattant de l'Europe
Uruguay – Amigo de Punta del Este, 1961

BOY SCOUTS OF AMERICA
Entered Scouting 1923; Eagle Scout 1926; various ranks and positions
Awards for Distinguished Service to Boyhood:
    Silver Beaver (11/1/50)
    Silver Antelope (10/19/51)
    Silver Buffalo (5/18/62)
    St. George Medal (1968) (First living non-Catholic to receive award)
    Distinguished Eagle Scout (1969)
Patron – World Scouting
Order of the Arrow
Knights of Dunamis
National Eagle Scout Association (charter member)
Alpha Phi Omega (Life Member) – National Executive Board, 1960-1963
Lone Indian Fellowship
    Member, Susquehannock Tribe – LIF

National Offices:
    Chairman, Advisory Council, 1970-1978
    National Treasurer, 1967-1970
    Assistant Treasurer, 1970-1975
    National Finance Committee, 1962-1973
        Chairman, 1967-1970
        Vice-Chairman, 1970-1973
    National Executive Board, 1959-1974
    National Executive Committee, 1962-1978
    National Court of Honor, 1966-
        Chairman, Distinguished Eagle Scout Award Committee, 1969-
    National Personnel and Training Committee, 1958-1973
        Chairman, 1962-1967
    National Supply Service Division Committee, 1953-
        Vice Chairman, 1965-1974
    National Explorer Committee, 1958-1963
    Civic Relationships Committee, 1959-1963
        Chairman, 1960-1963

Employee Benefits Committee, 1960-1967
    Chairman, 1963-1967
Johnston Historical Museum Committee, 1965-1978
Regional Offices:
    Region 11 Executive Committee, 1949-1953
        Vice-Chairman, 1952-1953
        Honorary Member, 1953
    Region 7 Executive Committee, 1956-1965
        Chairman, 1959-1962
        Honorary Member, 1965
    Region 3 Executive Committee, 1965
Local Offices:
    Portland Area Council (Oregon), Executive Board, 1946-1953
        President, 1949-1951
    Thatcher Woods Area Council (Oak Park, Illinois), Executive Board, 1956-60
        President, 1959-1960
    Chicago Area Council, Executive Board, 1957-1960
        Advisory Board, 1960-1974
    Chief Okemos Council (Lansing, Michigan), Executive Board, 1962-1965
    Lehigh Council (Allentown, Pennsylvania), Executive Board, 1965-1969
        Vice President, 1965-1969
    Minsi Trails Council, Executive Board, 1969-1974
        Chairman, Advisory Board, 1970-1976
    Mason-Dixon Council (Hagerstown, Md.), Executive Board, 1967-1974
    Columbia-Pacific Council, Honorary Vice President, 1970-1978
AMERICAN HUMANICS FOUNDATION
    President, 1956-1958
    Chairman of the Board, 1968-1969
    Chairman Emeritus, 1969-
    Chairman, Administrative Committee, 1959-1969
    Chairman, Executive Committee, 1962-1969
    Chairman Awards Committee, 1959-1970
    Member, Student Loan Board of Managers, 1959-1970
    Patron
    Honorary Life Member
    Exemplar Award, 1978
ORGANIZATIONS
Technical
    Society of Automotive Engineers
        Chairman, Oregon Section, 1942-1944
        Life Member
        Motor Vehicle Manufacturers Association
        Secretary, 1965-1967

Vice President, 1967-1968
Secretary, 1969-1970
Heavy Duty Truck Manufacturers Association
   Founder Automotive Hall of Fame
Life Member
Distinguished Service Citation, 1968
Board of Directors, 1968-1974
Member of the Executive Committee, 1970-1974
Treasurer, 1971-1974
Elected to Automotive Hall of Fame in 1982
Board of Trustees, 1974 to present
American Society for Quality Control – Honorary
Society for the Advancement of Management, 1968-1974
American Historical Truck Museum-Library
   Hall of Fame Founder, 1973
Executive Vice President

Civic
State of Indiana, Council of the Sagamores of the Wabash
Tennessee Squire
Honorary Citizen
   Kansas City, Missouri, 1959
   New Orleans, Louisiana, 1962
   Kenner, Louisiana, 1965
   Lubbock, Texas, 1967
   Artesia, New Mexico, 1969
   Honorable Knight, Royal Rosarians, Portland, Oregon
   Boiling Springs, North Carolina, 1973
   Greenville, South Carolina, 1973

Keys to the City
Tacoma, Washington, 1950
Kansas City, Missouri, 1956
New Orleans, Louisiana, 1962
Kenner, Louisiana, 1969
Allentown, Pennsylvania, 1965
Cortland, New York, 1967
Las Vegas, Nevada, 1967
Metropolitan Miami, Florida, 1968
St. Paul, Minnesota, 1968
Artesia, New Mexico, 1969
Abilene, Texas, 1970
Pennsylvania State Chamber of Commerce – Director, 1966, 1971
Allentown – Lehigh County Chamber of Commerce
   Distinguished Service Award, 1968

Cortland, New York Chamber of Commerce
  Distinguished Service Award, 1968
Latin Chamber of Commerce, Miami
  Distinguished Service Award, 1969

United Fund
  Campaign Chairman, Greater Lansing, 1964
  Member of Board of Directors, Lehigh County, 1966-1970
  Chairman, Major Firms Division, Lehigh County, 1966
  Campaign Chairman, Lehigh County, 1967
  President, Lehigh County, 1968
  Member, National Citizens Committee United Fund Community
    Campaigns of American, 1969-1970
  Y.M.C.A. Member of Board of Directors, Allentown, 1966-1968
  U.S. Treasury Bond Drive (Share in America) County Chairman, 1969
  Governor's Committee of 100,000 Pennsylvanians for Economic Growth
    Chairman, 1968-1970
  Allentown Art Museum – Trustee and Director, 1966-1972
  Allentown Symphony – Director
  Lehigh County Historical Society
  Greater Philadelphia Chamber of Commerce 1973 Transportation Award
  Foreign Traders Assoc. of Philadelphia – 31st annual
    Man of the Year Award, 1974
  International Automotive Hall of Fame – 1972
  Allentown Jaycees
    20th Anniversary Boss's Appreciation Award, 1967
    Allentown Patriots
      Outstanding Citizens Award, 1966
      Honorary Life Award
  Borough Brothers of Brush, Coplay, Pennsylvania, 1969
  Junior Achievement of Lehigh Valley, Inc., 1966
  St. Patrick's Day Committee Life Member, 1967
    Parade Grand Marshal, 1968
  Police Chief's Association, Middle Eastern Pennsylvania
    Honorary Life Member, 1967
  Fraternal Order of Police, Allentown, Pennsylvania, – Associate Member
  Traffic Club of Lehigh Valley, Inc.
    Appreciation Award, 1966
  Allentown Sports Show
    Eminent Sportsman Award, 1970
  American Educational & Historical Film Center – Advisory Committee, 1969
  Pop Warner Little Scholars, Inc. – Board of Directors, 1969-1976
  All American Eleven, 1971
  Goodwill Industries

National Good Scout Award, 1969
Advisory Board of Directors, 1970
Citizens Committee for Postal Reform, 1969
Lehigh County Fish & Game Protective Association, Honorary Member, 1969
Wisdom Hall of Fame – Award of Honor, 1969
B'nai B'rith National Humanitarian Award, 1970
United Jewish Appeal Humanitarian Award, 1971
Pearl S. Buck Foundation, Advisory Board of Directors, 1971
Friends of the Chapel of Four Chaplains, Inc. (Life Member)
Community Services of Pennsylvania, Trustee, 1969-1974
National Committee for Vincent T. Lombardi Memorial Sports Center, Fordham University, 1971
National Advisory Committee to the Vincent T. Lombardi Cancer Research Center, Georgetown University, 1971
The Swedish Colonial Society, 1971
American Academy of Achievement, Golden Plate Award, 1972
Lehigh Valley Society for Crippled Children & Adults Chairman Easter Seal Campaign, 1972
Religious Heritage of America
Business Leader of the Year Award, 1972
Pennsylvania Exchange Club – Citizen of the Year Award, 1972
Lehigh County Vocational Technical School – General Advisory Council, 1973-1974
Pittsburgh's Morningside Bulldogs, Inc. – Honorary Advisory Board, 1973
Golden Slipper Club – Annual Achievers Award, 1973
Horatio Alger Award, 1974
Horatio Alger Award Committee, 1974-
President, Horatio Alger Award Committee, 1978-

Fraternal
South Gate Lodge No. 182, A.F. & A.M. (Life Member)
South Gate Chapter No. 149, O.E.S. (Life Member)
Friendship Chapter No. 48 R.A.M. (Life Member)
Multnomah Council No. 11, R.S.M. (Life Member)
Oregon Commandery No. 1 K.T. (Life Member)
Oregon Consistory, 32nd Degree (Life Member) 1944-1967
Honorary Member, 1970
Lehigh Consistory, 32nd Degree (Life Member) 1967- 33rd Degree, 1971
Tall Cedars of Lebanon, Allentown Forest No. 41 (Life Member)
Tall Cedar at Sight
Royal Order of Scotland (Life Member)
Al Kader Temple (Life Member)

International Association of Pipe Smoker's Clubs, Inc., 1973
American Security Council, National Advisory Board
American Truck Historical Society, 1973
   Honorary Member
El Khurafeh Temple, Saginaw, Michigan
   Honorary Member
   Ambassador, 1962
Rajah Temple, Reading, Pennsylvania
   Honorary Member, 1965
   Ambassador at Large
   Oriental Band – Honorary Member, 1968
Royal Order of Jesters
   Chicago Court No. 48, 1957-1966
   Allentown Court 195, 1966-1975
Order of DeMolay – Honorary Legion of Honor
Loyal Order of the Moose (Life Member)
   Allentown Elk of the Year 1970
Woodmen of the World
Independent Order of Foresters

Social

L'Ordre Mondial des Gourmets Propagandistes (Membre Foundateur)
Confrerie de la Chaine des Rotisseurs (Senechal d'Honneur du Michigan)
Bailli, Lehigh Valley Chapitre, 1968-1970
Bailli Delegue des U.S.A., 1973-1975
Bailli Honoraire des U.S.A., 1976-
Membre Conseil Magistral, 1974-1976
   Membre Honoraire du Conseil Magistral, 1976-
Bailli Delegue du Northeast des U.S.A., 1971-1972
Bailli Delegue du Southeast des U.S.A., 1976-
Confrerie des Chevaliers du Tastevin-en-Main, 1976-
Commandeur, 1973-
Commanderie d'Amerique, 1971-1976
Acadamie de Gastornomie Brillat-Savarin
Membre Academicien, Fauteuil 22
The Culinary Institute of America, Fellow, 1972

Miscellaneous

Newcomen Society of North America
Oldtime Boxer's Association – Ring 23 – Honorary Life Member, 1966
Oregon Boxer (Dog) Club, Honorary Life member, President
Giant Schnauzer Club of America, Inc. (Giant of the Year, 1964)
Giant Schnauzer Club of Mid-America
Lehigh County Humane Society (Life Member)

National Rifle Association of America (Life Member)
North American Vexillological Association (Life Member)
Intercontinental Biographical Association (Life Member)
CLUBS
Allentown, Pennsylvania: Rotary Club – Honorary Member
  Paul Harris Fellow
Chicago, Illinois: Union League Club
  71 Club (Charter)
Residence: Sebring, Florida

Bibliography

"**In Allentown Ceremonies Sept. 26.**" *The Morning Herald.* Hagerstown, Maryland. 17 September 1970. Digital image, Ancestry.com, http://www.ancestry.com (Accessed 2-22-2012).

Annual Reports to Congress. Boy Scouts of America. 1953-1975. Digital images, GenealogyBank. http://www.genealogybank.com (Accessed 1-5-2013).

"**Anthems to Fete Palm Sunday.**" *The Oregonian.* Portland, Oregon. 9 April 1949: page 5. Digital image, GenealogyBank. http://www.genealogybank.com (Accessed 10-11-2012).

Barbarosh, Roslyn. "**Man Serves Two Masters – A Bulldog and The U.S. Flag**" Associated Press. Trenton (New Jersey) *Evening News.* 19 September 1971. Digital image, GenealogyBank. http://www.genealogybank.com (Accessed 10-11-2012).

Bartlett, Kay. "**Zenon Hansen of Mack Truck – a Real Bulldog.**" Associated Press. *Cleveland (Ohio) Plain Dealer.* 15 April 1973. Digital image, GenealogyBank. http://www.genealogybank.com (Accessed 10-11-2012).

Bauder, Donald C. "**Knievel Plugs Candy, Trucks For A Price.**" *San Diego Union.* 6 September 1974: page 67. Digital image, GenealogyBank. http://www.genealogybank.com (Accessed 10-11-2012).

Certificate of Marriage, 1933, American Consular Service. National Archives and Records Administration; Washington, D.C.; Marriage Reports in State Department Decimal Files, 1910-1949; Record Group: 59, General Records of the Department of State, 1763 - 2002; Series ARC ID: 2555709; Series MLR Number: A1, Entry 3001; Series Box Number: 504; File Number: 133. Digital image, Ancestry.com, http://www.ancestry.com (Accessed 1-28-2013). Zenon Hansen marriage to Margareta Marti.

"**Citizens Respond To Generals' Plight.**" Associated Press. *The News-Palladium.* Benton Harbor, Michigan. 5 December 1964. Digital image, Ancestry.com, http://www.ancestry.com (Accessed 2-24-2012).

Cleary, John J. "**White Motor VP Resigns to Pilot Mack Trucks, Inc.**" *Cleveland Plain Dealer.* 8 January 1965: page 24. Digital image, GenealogyBank. http://www.genealogybank.com (Accessed 10-11-2012).

"**Club to Hear of A-Bombing.**" *The Oregonian.* Portland, Oregon. 9 December 1946: page 6. Digital image, GenealogyBank. http://www.genealogybank.com (Accessed 10-11-2012).

Cook County Clerk Genealogy Records. Cook County Clerk's Office, Chicago, IL: Cook County Clerk, 2008. Marriage license: 5CB330D1-3485-4C8C-94B0-68FA287688EE. File number: 2338687. Digital record, Ancestry.com. Cook County, Illinois Marriage Index, 1930-1960. http://www.ancestry.com (Accessed 1-28-2013). Zenon Hansen marriage to Juanita. K. Moilanen.

Cook, Joan. "**Zenon C.R. Hansen, 81, Leader Who Restored Life to Mack Trucks.**" *The New York Times.* 23 October 1990. Digital image, Ancestry.com, http://www.ancestry.com (accessed 2012).

CPI Inflation Calculator. U.S Department of Labor, Bureau of Labor Statistics. http://data.bls.gov/cgi-bin/cpicalc.pl (Accessed 1-29-2013).

Doane College. www.doane.edu. (Accessed 1-28-2013).

"**Eagle Scout services honor 13 new members.**" *Syracuse Herald-Journal.* 2 December 1968: page 24. Digital image, Ancestry.com, http://www.ancestry.com (Accessed 2-22-2012).

Elby, David and Myers Jr., Paul. "**Lone Bear. H. Roe Bartle.**" U.S. Scouting Service Project. www.usscouts.org/honorsociety/lonebear.asp (Accessed 1-28-2013).

"**Ex-Portlander Returns With Boost for Scouts.**" *The Oregonian*. Portland, Oregon. 17 May 1962: page 54. Digital image, GenealogyBank. http://www.genealogybank.com (Accessed 10-11-2012).

Finch & McCullouch's Aurora (Illinois) City Directory, 1936. Page 126. Ancestry.com. U.S. City Directories, 1821-1989. Digital image, Ancestry.com, http://www.ancestry.com (Accessed 1-28-2013). Zenon Hansen's residence.

"**Guard Hearing Opens Despite All Objections.**" Associated Press. *The News-Palladium*. Benton Harbor, Michigan. 16 February 1965. Digital image, Ancestry.com, http://www.ancestry.com (Accessed 2-24-2012).

"**Hansen Honored with St. George.**" *The Morning Herald*. Hagerstown, Maryland. 16 May 1968. Digital image, Ancestry.com, http://www.ancestry.com (Accessed 2-22-2012).

"**Hansen tells Origin of Mack's Bulldog.**" *Times-Picayune*. New Orleans, Louisiana. 19 June 1965: page 21. Digital image, GenealogyBank. http://www.genealogybank.com (Accessed 10-11-2012).

Hansen, Zenon C.R. **The Legend of the Bulldog.** New York: The Newcomen Society of North America. Published version of Hansen's speech to the Society in Philadelphia, Pennsylvania, on 16 January 1974.

Hansen, Zenon C.R. **Personal memo regarding his early childhood** and refuting a contention that he was a descendent of John Hanson, first U.S. president under the Articles of Confederation. Held by Doane College, Crete, Nebraska.

"**Has His World By The Seat Of Its Pants.**" *Daily Mail*. Hagerstown, Maryland. 2 May 1972. Digital Image, Ancestry.com, http://www.ancestry.com (Accessed 2-22-2012).

Hibbing Chamber of Commerce. "**Historical information.**" http://www.hibbing.org/historical.php (Accessed 1-29-2013.)

"**The History of the National Eagle Scout Association.**" National Eagle Scout Association. 2008 Eagle Scout Directory: page xxviii.

Holtzman, Stan. **Big Rigs. The Complete History of the American Semi Truck**. 2001, MBI Publishing Co., St. Paul, Minnesota. Pages 31-33. Digital images, Google Books. http://books.google.com/books?id=FaJgCm4YXS0C&pg=PA32&lpg=PA32&dq=history+of+Diamond+T+Trucks&source=bl&ots=35IW3MHU7v&sig=plFn2rEGLV8okCfVk8AA3fgun2A&hl=en&sa=X&ei=CAkMUZLYO6jcyQGD_YC4AQ&ved=0CDQQ6AEwATgK#v=onepage&q=history%20of%20Diamond%20T%20Trucks&f=false (Accessed 2-1-2013).

Horatio Alger Association. www.horatioalger.org. (Accessed 1-28-2013).

Interview with Thomas Haggai by Steve Myers. 21 September 2012. Held by The Zenon C.R. Hansen Foundation, AMG National Trust Bank, Greenwood Village, Colorado.

Interview with Earl Wright by Steve Myers. 14 February 2012. Held by The Zenon C.R. Hansen Foundation, AMG National Trust Bank, Greenwood Village, Colorado.

Interview with Carrie Petr by Steve Myers. 28 February 2012. Held by The Zenon C.R. Hansen Foundation, AMG National Trust Bank, Greenwood Village, Colorado.

Interview with Jay Fennell by Steve Myers. 28 February 2012. Held by The Zenon C.R. Hansen Foundation, AMG National Trust Bank, Greenwood Village, Colorado.

Interview with Cammie Schwartz by Steve Myers. 27 February 2012. Held by The Zenon C.R. Hansen Foundation, AMG National Trust Bank, Greenwood Village, Colorado.

Iowa State Census, 1925. Ancestry.com. Iowa, State Census Collection, 1836-1925 [database on-line]. Provo, UT, USA: Ancestry.

com Operations Inc, 2007. Original data: Microfilm of Iowa State Censuses, 1856, 1885, 1895, 1905, 1915, 1925 as well various special censuses from 1836-1897 obtained from the State Historical Society of Iowa via Heritage Quest. (Accessed 1-28-2013).

"**Mack agrees to sell Soviets machinery, know-how.**" *Morning Herald*. Hagerstown, Maryland. 18 June 1971. Digital image, Ancestry.com, http://www.ancestry.com (Accessed 2-24-2012).

"**Major Breakthrough in Diesels Produced by Mack Truck Inventors.**" *The Daily Mail*. Hagerstown, Maryland. 17 October 1966. Digital image, Ancestry.com, http://www.ancestry.com (Accessed 2-24-2012).

Mack Trucks, Inc. History. Funding Universe. http://www.fundinguniverse.com/company-histories/mack-trucks-inc-history/.

The Maroon & White 1927. Central High School yearbook, Sioux City, Iowa. digital images, Ancestry.com, http://www.ancestry.com (Accessed 1-28-2013). Pages 63, 134, 144, 164, 166-167.

Minnesota Humanities Center. Hibbing population in 1910. http://minnesotahumanities.org/Resources/Iron%20Range%20Jews%20Timeline.pdf.

Munson, Thomas. "**The Unbuilt Sioux City**. Sioux City Preservation Committee. http://www.siouxcityhp.org/articles/6-the-unbuilt-sioux-city.html (Accessed 1-29-2013).

New York, Passenger Lists, 1820-1957. Year: 1935; Arrival: New York, United States; Microfilm Serial: T715; Microfilm Roll: 5684; Line: 10; Page Number: 22. Digital image, Ancestry.com, http://www.ancestry.com (Accessed 1-28-2013).

Nixon Presidential Materials Staff. Tape Subject Log: Conversation No. 515-2. 9 June 1971. (Rev. 10/08) Digital image, Ancestry.com, http://www.ancestry.com (Accessed 2-22-2012).
"**Officers in Guard Case Ask Salary**." United Press International. *Traverse City (Michigan) Record-Eagle*. 23 February 1965. Digital image, Ancestry.com, http://www.ancestry.com (Accessed 2-24-2012).

Polk's Gary (Lake County, Indiana) City Directory, 1937. Page 173. Ancestry.com. U.S. City Directories, 1821-1989. Digital image, Ancestry.com, http://www.ancestry.com (Accessed 1-28-2013). Zenon Hansen's residence.

Polk's Kelso and Longview (Washington) City Directory, 1946. Page 281. Ancestry.com. U.S. City Directories, 1821-1989. Digital image, Ancestry.com, http://www.ancestry.com (Accessed 1-28-2013). Juanita Kellogg Moilanen's residence.

Polk's Portland (Oregon) City Directory, 1943-44. Pages, 695, 1180. Ancestry.com. U.S. City Directories, 1821-1989. Digital image, Ancestry.com, http://www.ancestry.com (Accessed 1-28-2013). Zenon and Lilian Hansen's residence and John and Juanita Moilanen's residence.

Polk's Portland (Oregon) City Directory, 1953. Pages 448, 753. Ancestry.com. U.S. City Directories, 1821-1989. Digital image, Ancestry.com, http://www.ancestry.com (Accessed 1-28-2013). Zenon and Lilian Hansen's residence and Juanita Moilanen's residence.

Potter, Richard M. "**The Full History of American Humanics Program**." Baruch College, School of Public Affairs, The City University of New York. www.baruch.cuny.edu/spa/academics/undergraduateprograms/AmericanHumanicsFullHistory.php. (Accessed 1-28-2013).

Pratt, Gary. "**Mack Truck Wizard Boosts Firm Output**." *The Oregonian*. Portland, Oregon. 1 March 1970: page 36. Digital image, GenealogyBank. http://www.genealogybank.com (Accessed 10-11-2012).

"**Prize Dogs Receive Awards As Judging Gets Underway**." *The Oregonian*. Portland, Oregon. 11 April 1948: page 66. Digital image, GenealogyBank. http://www.genealogybank.com (Accessed 10-11-2012).

Pryce, Dick. "**The First Distinguished Eagle**." *Scouting*. January-February 1988: pages 8, 42. **Resumes of Zenon C.R. Hansen**. Held by The Zenon C.R. Hansen Foundation, AMG National Trust Bank, Greenwood Village, Colorado.

Riedy, Roy. "**Zenon and Marilyn Hansen – Generous Friends of HLT**." Highland Little Theater, Sebring, Florida. www.highlandslittletheatre.org. (Accessed 1-31-2012).

Shope, Dan. "**Hansen Eulogized as Good Scout**." *The Morning Call*. Allentown, Pennsylvania. 6 November 1990. http://articles.mcall.com/1990-11-06/news/2772431_1_mack-trucks-boy-scout-hansen-s-death. (Accessed 1-28-2013).

Shulz, Blaine "**Activist intimidation' kills Soviet truck deal**." *The Oregonian*. Portland, Oregon. Digital image, GenealogyBank. http://www.genealogybank.com (Accessed 10-12-2012).

"**Signal Oil Link With Mack Trucks Gets Boards' Okay**." *Boston Herald*. 5 May 1967: page 16. Digital image, GenealogyBank. http://www.genealogybank.com (accessed 10-12-2012).

"**The Story of Zenon C. R. Hansen, Truck Man Extraordinary**." 20 October 1964. Mock eight-page *Life* magazine issued by Diamond T Trucks Inc. at banquet honoring Hansen for 20 years in truck industry. Held by Doane College, Crete, Nebraska.

"**Super Food Services, Inc. History**." Funding Universe. http://www.fundinguniverse.com/company-histories/super-food-services-inc-history/ (Accessed 1-28-2013).

"**$340,000 given to MSU Young Fund**." United Press International. *The Holland Evening Sentinel*. Holland, Michigan. 26 December 1963. Digital image, Ancestry.com, http://www.ancestry.com (Accessed 1-28-2013).

"**Transportation Museum Rolls Into Allentown**." Trailer/Body Builders. 25 March 2008. http://www.trailer-bodybuilders.com. (Accessed 2-1-12).

Trierweiler, Dick. "**Diamond T History**." Diamond T Classics. http://www.diamondtclassics.com/modules.php?op=modload&name=News&file=article&sid=105 (Accessed 2-1-2013).

"**Trucking Management Profile: The Man Who Came to Dinner**." Unknown publisher. 1964. Reprint held by Doane College, Crete, Nebraska.

1910 U.S. Census, Hibbing, St. Louis County, Minnesota; Roll: T624_723; Page: 29A; Enumeration District: 0235; Image: FHL microfilm: 1374736. National Archives microfilm publication; digital image, Ancestry.com, http://www.ancestry.com (Accessed 1-28-2013). Zenon Hansen's place of residence.

1920 U.S. Census, Sioux City Precinct 2, Woodbury County, Iowa; Roll: T625_520; Page: 4A; Enumeration District: 198; Image: 368. National Archives microfilm publication; digital image, Ancestry.com, http://www.ancestry.com (Accessed 1-28-2013). Zenon Hansen's place of residence.

1920 U.S. Census, School District 13, Roosevelt County, Montana; Roll: T625_975; Page: 1B; Enumeration District: 194; Image: 405. National Archives microfilm; digital image, Ancestry.com, http://www.ancestry.com (Accessed 1-28-2013). Juanita Kellogg's place of residence.

About the Author

Steve Myers is an award-winning journalist from Denver, Colorado. He has worked in reporting and editing roles for the Rocky Mountain News (Denver), Contra Costa Times (California) Medford Mail Tribune (Oregon), Eugene Register-Guard (Oregon) and Springfield News (Oregon). A native of Eugene, he graduated from the University of Oregon in 1981.

CPSIA information can be obtained at www.ICGtesting.com
Printed in the USA
LVOW08*0733310315

432638LV00003B/4/P